T0161454

Dreaming of Fallen Blossoms

Dreaming of Fallen Blossoms

Tune Poems of Su Dong-Po

Translations by Yun Wang

White Pine Press / Buffalo, New York

White Pine Press
P.O. Box 236
Buffalo, NY 14201
www.whitepine.org

Acknowledgments:
Grateful acknowledgment is made to the following journals in which these poems, some of them in earlier versions (or in parts), first appeared:

Confluence:
"Butterfly and Flowers: Blossoms fade in withered red and apricots are tiny, " "The Song of the Cave Celestial: Skin of ice and bones of jade"

(Acknowledgments continue on page 205.)

NYSCA   ART WORKS.

Cover Image by Elaine LaMattina

Printed and bound in the United States of America.

Library of Congress Control Number: 2018947135

ISBN 978-1-945680-27-4

In memory of my father Wang Zheng-Chu (1927-2011),
my childhood mentor in classical Chinese poetry

以此纪念从小教我古诗词的父亲
王正初 (1927-2011)

Contents

江城子 / From the River City

洞仙歌 / The Song of the Cave Celestial

∽

Introduction

The Song Dynasty (960-1279 A.D.) was founded by Tai Zu (the Founding Emperor) Zhao Kuang-Yin (赵匡胤, 927-976 A.D.). He led generals in a successful coup when the emperor of the Latter Zhou Dynasty died and was succeeded by his seven-year old son. To prevent the warlords from dividing up the country, and the corrupt associates of the imperial household from abusing their power, Tai Zu placed scholars above generals in the social order, concentrated power in the central government, and weakened the power of the generals. This created a prosperous and unprecedented open society, but also had the unintended consequence of making the empire vulnerable to invaders and eventually led to its demise. Song Dynasty was a golden age in Chinese history in economy, commerce, culture, education, science, and creativity.

Su Dong-Po (苏东坡) was born on January 8, 1037, during the peak of this golden age, in Meishan of Meizhou (now Meizhou City in Sichuan Province). He died on August 24, 1101. He was also known as Su Shi (苏轼) and Su Zi-Zhan (苏子瞻). In ancient China, an educated man would have three different names. The private name (名) was given to him at birth. When he grew older, the public name (字) was given to him as the name by which he should be known in public. When he became an adult, he would acquire one or more honorary names (号). Su's private name was Shi. His public name was Zi-Zhan. His favorite and most frequently used honorary name was Dong-Po Ju Shi (Hermit of East Hill), which he gave himself later in life. He is generally known as Su Dong-Po in China today.

Su Dong-Po came from an illustrious literary family, descended from the early Tang Dynasty prime minister and poet Su Wei-Dao (苏味道, 648-705 A.D.). Su Dong-Po, his brother Su Zhe (苏辙, referred to by his public name Zi-You 子由 in Dong-Po's writings), and their father Su Xun (苏洵) are the famous Three Su's from the Song Dynasty in Chinese history. Dong Po's mother was from the prominent Chen (程) family in Meishan. She had a profound influence on Dong-Po. When Dong-Po was ten years old, his father began traveling extensively as a scholar while his mother schooled him.

The system of selecting prospective government officials through exams was established during the Tang Dynasty (618-907 A.D.). The Song emperors not only appointed scholars who placed the highest in the final official exam to prominent positions in the central government, but also sent them out to the provinces to rule as governors on three-year terms, to ensure control of the provinces and prevent abuses of power by the governors.

In 1057, Su Xun and his two sons, the twenty year old Dong-Po and the eighteen-year old Zi-You, left their home in the remote and rural Meishan, and sailed east down the Yangtze River, to take the official exams in the capitol. The main examiner was the leader of the literary world at the time, Ou-Yang Xiu (欧阳修), who was amazed by Dong-Po's literary gift and refreshingly creative style. With Eu-Yang Xiu's praise, Dong-Po became famous in the capitol city overnight. Each poem he composed became an instant hit and was widely circulated. However, before the three Su's were able to show their worth in the final official exam, they received news that Dong-Po's mother passed away. The three of them immediately set off toward home. They returned to the capital in 1061 after observing the customary three years of mourning for her. Dong-Po placed first in the final official exam that year, which began his career as a government official. He was first appointed to the position of inspector general in Dali (大理) for four years, then returned to the capitol to preside over the Appeals Court.

In 1066, Su Xun passed away due to an illness in the capitol. Dong-Po and Zi-You accompanied his body home, along with that of Dong-Po's first wife, Wang Fu (王弗), who had died the previous year. After observing three years of mourning for his father, and marrying Wang Fu's first cousin Wang Run-Zhi (王闰之), Dong-Po returned to the court. He found that things had changed. The new Prime Minister Wang An-Shi (王安石) began reforms that shook up the count. Many of Dong-Po's friends, including his mentor Eu-Yang Xiu, disagreed with the reforms, and were forced to leave the capitol. In 1071, Dong-Po presented a letter to the emperor expounding the problems caused by the reforms. This angered Wang An-Shi, who instructed the Imperial Judge (御使) to criticize Dong-Po in front of the emperor. This prompted Dong-Po to request that the emperor appoint him to a position away from the capitol. The emperor appointed Dong-Po the judge of Hangzhou (杭州) in 1071, where he stayed until transferred to Mizhou (密州) as its governor in 1074. Before leaving Hangzhou, Dong-Po's wife Run-Zhi brought a twelve-year old girl, Wang Chao-Yun (王朝云), into the family as her maidservant.

Chao-Yun would play an important role in Dong-Po's life years later.

Dong-Po was transferred from Mizhou to Xuzhou (徐州) as its governor in 1077, and then to Huzhou (湖州) as its governor in 1079. Everywhere he went, he changed government policies to benefit the people, and the people loved him.

Dong-Po was about forty-two years old when he became the governor of Huzhou in 1079. Soon after his arrival, he composed a letter to the emperor thanking him for the appointment. This was part of the bureaucratic ritual, but Dong-Po wrote a personalized letter. In the letter, he stated that he was too stupid to fit in with the times, incapable of following the reformers' footsteps, and too old to make trouble, but perhaps he could shepherd the people instead. These words delighted the reformers, who seized the opportunity to accuse him of harboring resentment and disloyalty toward the emperor, disrespecting the emperor, mocking the central government and wishing it ill. From Dong-Po's vast number of poems, they picked lines here and there that they deemed sarcastic toward the emperor to support their accusations. Three months after becoming the governor of Huzhou, Dong-Po was arrested, and brought to the capitol to face a death sentence. Dozens of his friends faced related charges. This was the famous "Crow Terrace Poetry Case (乌台诗案)" from the Song Dynasty. The Crow Terrace referred to the Imperial Judge's Terrace, where crows resided in cypress trees all year around.

The Crow Terrace Poetry Case was the turning point in Dong-Po's life. The reformers were determined to have Dong-Po put to death. Many others, including senior officials with similar political views as well as reformers who admired his literary talent, tried to rescue Dong-Po. Eventually, he was saved by the retired reformer Wang An-Shi, who wrote to the emperor wondering why an enlightened dynasty would kill gifted scholars. This worked since the founding emperor of the Song Dynasty, Tai Zu, made the rule that eminent scholars who held government positions were exempt from the death sentence.

After one hundred and three days in prison and nearly executed several times, Dong-Po was released, and demoted to Huangzhou (黄州) in 1080, as a minor official with no actual power, under the close watch of local officials. Dong-Po was depressed and lost interest in politics when arriving in Huangzhou in the winter in early 1080. His meager pay was not enough for his family to live on, so he obtained government permission through a friend to farm an abandoned military campground on a hill east of the city. He began calling himself Dong-Po Ju Shi (Hermit of East Hill), an honorary name by which he is still generally known today.

In 1084, Dong-Po was transferred to Ruzhou (汝州). It was an arduous long journey from Huangzhou to Ruzhou. Dong-Po's infant son became ill on the way and died. Devastated by this loss, and out of money to pay for the traveling expenses, Dong-Po wrote to the emperor requesting a delay of the appointment, and asked for permission to go live in Changzhou (常州). This was granted. Dong-Po and his family lived for a while in beautiful Changzhou, where Dong-Po planned to grow old.

In 1085, a new emperor ascended the throne, and Empress Dowager Gao (高太后) assumed power on account of the tender age of the emperor. The reformers were replaced by the old party in the government. Dong-Po was soon summoned back to the capitol, and promoted to the position of Master of the Imperial Academy (翰林学士), the most prominent advisor to the emperor. However, Dong-Po discovered that the new government persecuted the reformers and abolished all reforms without differentiating those that worked from those that did not. He exposed the corruption of the new government to the emperor, and earned the enmity of the new top officials in the government, who tried to persecute him. Dong-Po again did not fit in, and once again asked the emperor to appoint him to a position away from the capitol.

In 1089, Dong-Po became the governor of Hangzhou. Due to years of neglect, the West Lake in Hangzhou was filled with mud and overgrown with weeds. This was detrimental to local agriculture, which depended on water from the West Lake for irrigation. The year after he took office, Dong-Po led the renovation of the West Lake to remove the mud and restore the water level, mobilizing over twenty thousand workers. He had three towers built to mark where the lake was deepest, and used the mud removed from the lake to build a long dam across the West Lake. The Su Dam (苏公堤) was connected by six bridges to allow both pedestrian and boat traffic, and lined by willows and flowering trees. "Three Towers in

Moonlight" and "Spring Dawn on the Su Dam" have since become two of the top ten scenic attractions in Hangzhou. He built two more dams later on west lakes elsewhere with similar benefits to the people, one in Yingzhou (颍州), and finally in Huizhou (惠州) where he donated his own funds to help build the dam.

Dong-Po was very happy in scenic and prosperous Hangzhou, but he was summoned back to court in 1091. Soon, because of political conflicts, he was sent out again as the governor, first of Yingzhou (颍州) in 1091, then to Yangzhou (扬州) in 1092, then to Dingzhou (定州) in 1093.

In 1093, the Empress Dowager Gao passed away, and the emperor Zhe Zong (哲宗) assumed power. Dong-Po's second wife Run-Zhi died that same year. The reformers were back in power, and Dong-Po was demoted to Huizhou (惠州) in 1094, as the deputy to the general of the border army. He was accompanied by Chao-Yun. Finally, in 1097, the sixty year old Dong-Po, who just lost Chao-Yun the previous year, was banished to the remote and desolate Danzhou (儋州) on Hainan Island (海南岛). It was said that during the Song Dynasty, banishment to Hainan was the fate for a government official that was only better than having your entire clan executed for your offenses. Dong-Po settled whole-heartedly in Danzhou, and considered it his second hometown. He built schools and nurtured scholarly discourse. Dong-Po was the cultural founder of Danzhou. There are villages, wells, fields, roads, bridges, even hats, and a dialect in Danzhou that are named after Dong-Po.

In 1100, the emperor Zhe Zong died without a son, and his brother became the new emperor Hui Zong (徽宗), who cleared Dong-Po's name, and restored him to his former position at the court. During his journey back north to the capitol in 1101, Dong-Po passed away in Changzhou at the age of sixty-four.

❧

Su Dong-Po represents the pinnacle of literary accomplishment from the Song Dynasty. He is credited with transforming ci (词, tune poem) from a minor form of poetry, written to match fixed tunes and often used to express amorous feelings, to a major form of poetry capable of expressing the full range of emotions and the human condition. It became the primary vessel for lyric poetry in classical Chinese poetry. While Dong-Po is famous for his regular poems (诗) and essays (文), he is most celebrated for his tune poems; they have placed him in Chinese history as one of the greatest poets. School children in China learn that the indispensable classics in poetry are Tang shi Song ci (唐诗宋词, Tang poems and Song tune poems). Li Bai (李白) and Du Fu (杜甫) are the grand masters of Tang shi; Su Dong-Po is the grand master of Song ci.

Tune poems were once written as lyrics to tunes, usually with contrived words that fit the tunes but made poor poetry. Dong-Po elevated tune poems to the same stature as regular poems by noting that they shared the same origin, and that tune poems were descended from regular poems. He held tune poems to the same artistic standards as regular poems, and demonstrated with his own work that tune poems can have distinct styles that reflect each poet's individual creativity. Dong-Po expanded the reach of tune poems by composing masterpieces about warriors, villagers, hunting, courtesans, monks, ancient ruins, contemplation of the meaning of life, etc., all beyond that of traditional tune poems. This was stunning and liberating to his contemporaries. Because tune poems were sung with music, they became more effective than traditional poems in their artistic power.

The main technique that Dong-Po used in revolutionizing the tune poem was to use it to express himself the same way he would a regular poem. He started the practice of using titles and epigraphs, as well as literary and historical allusions. The title and epigraph provided the background, and sometimes a backstory, for the tune poem, enriching its content. The allusions added depth to the tune poems by enabling the expression of complex thoughts and emotions in a condensed form.

One frequent theme in Dong-Po's tune poems is that life is a dream. This is a reflection of his philosophical outlook, as well as his Buddhist and Taoist leanings. The realization that life is a dream did not lead him to negate life, but compelled him to transcend the slings and arrows of fate, as well as the busy seeking of fame and fortune. He adapted to whatever situation he was tossed into, went with the flow, and enjoyed the journey, with plenty of poetry, friends, and wine. He was an optimist who was empathic to suffering, and worked hard to make life better for others. He was sensitive to beauty in nature and in people. He navigated the complexities of life and the world, and dreamed of sailing the Milky Way.

Dong-Po was generous and fearless, and possessed a great sense of humor. He was also a master calligrapher and painter. This enabled him to see the world through a painter's eyes, capturing precise and vivid details. These qualities help explain the timeless appeal of his poems across the centuries.

The sixty-six tune poems by Su Dong-Po collected in this volume were translated from early 1990s to 2015, when the book manuscript took form. Continuous revisions followed until spring 2018. The translator grew up in China reading and reciting these poems in the original Chinese. These poems have been chosen because they hold spiritual resonance with the translator across the thousand year time span. Most of the poems in this volume are appearing in English translation for the first time. Notes have been added to make this bilingual volume a useful reference for students of Chinese, as well as of poetry.

Dong-Po was very close to his only brother, Zi-You, who was two years younger. The two of them had similar political careers, and similar literary styles; Zi-You was heavily influenced by his brother. Many of Dong-Po's poems were written to Zi-You, or in response to poems by Zi-You. A number of poems in this collection are such examples.

Dong-Po had numerous friends, with whom he shared wine, and exchanged poems. Many poems collected here are dedicated to such friends.

Three women helped shape Dong-Po's personal life, although they were often not explicitly named in his poems. Unlike the majority of women in Chinese history who are only known by their family names, all three women are remembered and honored today with their full names for their roles in Dong-Po's life.

Dong-Po married his first wife, Wang Fu 王弗 (1039-1065 A.D.), when she was sixteen and he was eighteen. Wang Fu was lovely, bright and learned, with a calm temperament. She liked to keep Dong-Po company when he studied. Dong-Po was delightfully surprised that she was able to help him in his studies with her broad knowledge of the classics. They were happy and deeply in love. She supported Dong-Po through his first hard years, but did not live long enough to enjoy his success. She died from an illness in the capitol when she was only twenty-six, leaving behind their six-year old son Su Mai (苏迈). She was buried near Dong-Po's parents on a hill, per instructions from Dong-Po's father before he died, in recognition of her loving care of Dong-Po and his parents during hardship. On that hill, Dong-Po and his brother Zi-You planted thirty thousand pine trees in memoriam. Dong-Po wrote one of his best known tune poems, "Ten years one alive one dead we share no light", when he dreamed of her, ten years after her death.

To care for his six-year old son Su Mai, Dong-Po remarried less than a year after Wang Fu died. He married Wang Fu's first cousin Wang Run-Zhi (王闰之, 1048-1093 A.D.), a trust-worthy country girl from a good family. She became a capable and content wife and mother, and treated her stepson Su Mai the same way as her own sons (Su Dai 苏迨 and Su Guo 苏过) with Dong-Po. She provided sanity and moral support, along with practical housekeeping, for the survival of the family, over the decades when Dong-Po was demoted and persecuted repeatedly. When Dong-Po was restored to glory and prominence in the capitol, Run-Zhi remained true to herself, maintained the same demeanor and personality. Dong-Po greatly admired her tenacity and was proud of her good sense, and referred to her in those contexts in many of his poems. Only one episode has become somewhat controversial historically. When Dong-Po was arrested because of the Crow Terrace Poetry Case, soldiers were sent to the Su household to search for his poems and writings to serve as incriminating evidence. Everyone in the house was terrified, and small children wailed. Run-Zhi stayed calm and burned most of Dong-Po's writings.

Run-Zhi died from an illness in 1093 in the capitol, when she was forty-five years old. She and Dong-Po had promised each other over the years to return together eventually to their hometown Mei-Shan. Dong-Po was deeply saddened by her early passing, and swore that he would repay her by sharing the same grave with her someday. Dong-Po's brother Zi-You wrote two elegies to mourn Run-Zhi, and made sure that she and Dong-Po were buried together in the end. A number of the tune poems collected here refer to the home-return dream that Run-Zhi and Dong-Po shared.

Dong-Po's soul-mate, Wang Chao-Yun (王朝云, 1062-1096 A.D.), came from a destitute family in Hangzhou. Dong-Po's wife Rui-Zhi bought her as a maidservant when she was twelve years old, when the Su family was about to depart Hangzhou for Mizhou in 1074. In popular legends, she was famed for her beauty, brilliance, singing and dancing; some even portrayed her as a famous courtesan in Hangzhou. No doubt she was exceptionally bright and beautiful, loved poetry and music, and adored Dong-Po, who came to adore her in return. She became Dong-Po's concubine (侍妾) when he was demoted to Huangzhou in 1080. She accompanied him to Huizhou in 1094, and died there in 1096.

Chao-Yun gave birth to Dong-Po's youngest son, Su Dun (苏遁) in 1083. Dong-Po was overjoyed, and wrote a famous poem celebrating his birth and naming. The following year, Dong-Po was transferred to Ruzhou, and forced to relocate the family over the long distance. That summer en route to Ruzhou, the infant got heat stroke and died in Chao-Yun's arms, because of the ineffective medicine from the doctor. Dong-Po was devastated, and blamed himself for the infant's bad luck, and for not having treated the infant himself as he had considerable medical skills (which he did not dare use since the ancients advised against treating one's own). Chao-Yun was crushed and lost the will to live at the time. Seventeen years later, Dong-Po died on the anniversary of his infant son's death.

Chao-Yun contracted an epidemic disease in Huizhou, and died at the age of thirty-four. She was a devout Buddhist. Dong-Po carried out her last wish and buried her in the pine grove of the Buddhist temple Xi Chan Si (栖禅寺).

Two stories reflect the deep understanding between Chao-Yun and Dong-Po. When Dong-Po worked in the capitol, one day he returned home from the imperial court with this question to the household: "What do you think is in my belly?" In the Chinese language, the belly is the figurative home of emotions and thoughts, etc. One maidservant said, "It is knowledge." Dong-Po shook his head. Another servant said, "It is filled with inner workings." Dong-Po shook his head again. Finally, Chao-Yun said, "The master scholar's belly is filled with unpopular ideas." Dong-Po burst into laughter holding his belly. He remarked, "The one who truly knows me, is none other than Chao-Yun." It has been said that after Dong-Po was demoted to Huizhou, Chao-Yun often sang his tune poem "Blossoms fade in withered red and apricots are tiny (花褪残红青杏小)" to him at his request. Chao-Yun often burst into tears singing "Willow catkins peel off branches in the wind", reminded of Dong-Po's fate of exile. Dong-Po comforted her by making jokes. After she died, Dong-Po could not bear to hear that tune poem again.

Su Dong-Po's tune poems, along with his legendary genius, charismatic personality, and storied life, have been woven into Chinese literary lore over the last thousand years. Only Li Bai has a similar reputation and stature in Chinese history and popular imagination; both of them have been called xian (仙), immortals who descended to earth to share their timeless poetry with the mortal world.

References:

[1] *History of the Song Dynasty – Biography of Su Shi* (宋史• 苏轼专)

[2] *Tune Poems from Tang and Song Dynasties: An Anthology With Commentary* (唐宋词鉴赏辞典), *Shanghai References Press* (上海辞书出版社), 1987

[3] *Selected Song Dynasty Tune Poems* (宋词选), edited by Hu Yun-Yi (胡云翼), Shanghai Classics Press (上海古籍出版社), 1978

[4] *Biography of Su Shi* (苏轼), Chinese Online Encyclopedia (百度百科), http://baike.baidu.com/view/2517.htm

[5] *Selected Works of Su Shi* (苏轼选集), edited by Wang Shui-Zhao (王水照), Shanghai Classics Press (上海古籍出版社), 1984

[6] *The Complete Collection of Song Dynasty Tune Poems* (宋词全集), International Culture Publishing Company (国际文化出版公司), 1995

[7] *The Life and Times of Su Tungpo*, by Lin Yutang, the John Day Company, New York, 1947

Dreaming of Fallen Blossoms

dié liàn huā
蝶恋花

一

chūn jǐng
春景

huā tuì cán hóng qīng xìng xiǎo
花褪残红青杏小
yàn zǐ fēi shí
燕子飞时
lù shuǐ rén jiā rào
绿水人家绕
zhī shàng liǔ mián chuī yòu shǎo
枝上柳绵吹又少
tiān yá hé chù wú fāng cǎo
天涯何处无芳草

qiáng lǐ qiū qiān qiáng wài dào
墙里秋千墙外道
qiáng wài xíng rén
墙外行人
qiáng lǐ jiā rén xiào
墙里佳人笑
xiào jiàn bù wén shēng jiàn xiāo
笑渐不闻声渐消
duō qíng què bèi wú qíng nǎo
多情却被无情恼

To the Tune of "Butterfly and Flowers"

I

Spring

Blossoms fade in withered red and apricots are tiny
Swallows appear in the sky
Green water swirls around houses
Willow catkins peel off branches in the wind
Where at the sky's edge does fragrant grass not thrive

Behind the wall is a swing beyond the wall is a trail
Beyond the wall a traveler passes
Behind the wall a girl laughs
The laughter wanes and the sound dies away
The heart is undone by the heartless

二

jì dé huà píng chū huì yù
记得画屏初会遇

hǎo mèng jīng huí
好梦惊回

wàng duàn gāo táng lù
望断高塘路

yàn zǐ shuāng fēi lái yòu qù
燕子双飞来又去

shā chuāng jǐ dù chūn guāng mù
纱窗几度春光暮

nà rì xiù lián xiāng jiàn chù
那日绣帘相见处

dī yǎn yáng xíng
低眼佯行

xiào zhěng xiāng yún lǚ
笑整香云缕

liǎn jìn chūn shān xiū bù yǔ
敛尽春山羞不语

rén qián shēn yì nán qīng sù
人前深意难轻诉

II

I recall our first meeting by the peacock screen
Startled from that beautiful dream
I obsess over the return path to Gaotang Terrace
Pairs of swallows have come and gone
Spring after spring has dimmed outside the gauze
    window

Our eyes met that day behind embroidered curtains
You lowered your eyes and pretended to leave
smiled and tucked back a scented strand of hair
You knit your brows into spring mountains
too shy to speak of all that could be between us

三

暮春别李公择

sù sù wú fēng huā zì duǒ
簌簌无风花自嚲
jì mò yuán lín
寂寞园林
liǔ lǎo yīng táo guò
柳老樱桃过
luò rì duō qíng hái zhào zuò
落日多情还照坐
shān qīng yī diǎn héng yún pò
山青一点横云破

lù jìn hé huí rén zhuǎn duò
路尽河回人转舵
jì lǎn yú cūn
系缆渔村
yuè àn gū dēng huǒ
月暗孤灯火
píng zhàng fēi hún zhāo chǔ xiē
凭仗飞魂招楚些
wǒ sī jūn chù jūn sī wǒ
我思君处君思我

III

Parting from Li Gong-Ze in Late Spring

Petals flutter down without wind
The garden trees are desolate
with willow fuzz and cherry blossoms gone
Tender sunset illuminates our sitting
A blue mountain breaks through horizon clouds

My path ends as your boat turns at the river's bend
It will drop anchor at a fishing village
where a single lamp flickers beneath dark moon
Both lost souls waiting to be summoned
we shall think of each other at the same instant

四

sòng chūn
送春

yǔ hòu chūn róng qīng gèng lì
雨后春容清更丽
zhǐ yǒu lí rén
只有离人
yōu hèn zhōng nán xǐ
幽恨终难洗
běi gù shān qián sān miàn shuǐ
北固山前三面水
bì qióng shū yōng qīng luó jì
碧琼梳拥青螺髻

yī zhǐ xiāng shū lái wàn lǐ
一纸乡书来万里
wèn wǒ hé nián
问我何年
zhēn gè chéng guī jì
真个成归计
bái shǒu sòng chūn pīn yī zuì
白首送春拼一醉
dōng fēng chuī pò qiān háng lèi
东风吹破千行泪

IV

Seeing Off Spring

The face of spring glows after rain
Only the man who left
has dusky regret that never washes off
The river hugs North Mountain on three sides
A jade comb holding dense spirals of hair

A letter came thousands of miles from home
asking which year
my plan to return would take place
I get drunk seeing off spring with white hair
East wind scatters a thousand lines of tears

五

mì zhōu shàng yuán
密州上元

dēng huǒ qián táng sān wǔ yè
灯火钱塘三五夜
míng yuè rú shuāng
明月如霜
zhào jiàn rén rú huà
照见人如画
zhàng dǐ chuī shēng xiāng tǔ shè
帐底吹笙香吐麝
gèng wú yī diǎn chén suí mǎ
更无一点尘随马

jìmò shān chéng rén lǎo yě
寂寞山城人老也
jī gǔ chuī xiāo
击鼓吹箫
zhà rù nóng sāng shè
乍入农桑社
huǒ lěng dēng xī shuāng lù xià
火冷灯稀霜露下
hūn hūn xuě yì yún chuí yě
昏昏雪意云垂野

V

Lantern Festival in Mizhou

Lights flooded Hangzhou on the Fifteenth Night
The moon crystallized in frost
illuminated women who stepped out from paintings
Someone played reed pipes behind musk-scented
    curtains
Not a grain of dust followed the horses

The desolate mountain town makes me old
Then drums beat and vertical flutes trill
I find myself in the farmers' harvest ritual
The fire burns out as lanterns scatter and cold dews
    descend
Clouds brood over an open field with a hint of snow

shuǐ diào gē tóu

水调歌头

一

huáng zhōu kuài zāi tíng zèng zhāng wò quán

黄州快哉亭赠张偓佺

luò rì xiù lián juǎn

落日绣帘卷

tíng xià shuǐ lián kōng

亭下水连空

zhī jūn wèi wǒ xīn zuò

知君为我新作

chuāng hù shī qīng hóng

窗户湿青红

cháng jì píng shān táng shàng

长记平山堂上

yī zhěn jiāng nán yān yǔ

欹枕江南烟雨

yǎo yǎo mò gū hóng

杳杳没孤鸿

rèn dé zuì wēng yǔ

认得醉翁语

shān sè yǒu wú zhōng

山色有无中

To the Tune of "The Water Song"

I

Presented to Zhang Wo-Quan at Crisp Wind Pavilion in Huangzhou

Roll up brocade curtains at sunset
Water blends with sky beneath the pavilion
I can see you redid this for me
Blue and vermilion paint still wet on windows
It reminds me of Pingshan Pavilion in Yangzhou
where I lounged to watch smoky Yangtze delta rain
A single goose flew into dark heights
Just as quoted by the Old Drunkard
"The mountains are there and not there"

yī qiān qǐng
一千顷
dōu jìng jìng
都镜净
dào bì fēng
倒碧峰
hū rán làng qǐ
忽然浪起
xiān wǔ yī yè bái tóu wēng
掀舞一叶白头翁
kān xiào lán tái gōng zǐ
堪笑兰台公子
wèi jiě zhuāng shēng tiān lài
未解庄生天籁
gāng dào yǒu cí xióng
刚道有雌雄
yī diǎn hào rán qì
一点浩然气
qiān lǐ kuài zāi fēng
千里快哉风

A crystal mirror spans
ten thousand acres
inverts jade peaks
Sudden billows rise
toss the leaf of a boat of a white-haired fisherman
I laugh thinking of young Lord Lan Tai
misreading Zhuang Zi's lore of heavenly flutes
elaborated on male wind and female wind
It takes a little air of vastness within
to ride a thousand miles of crisp wind

二

丙辰中秋，欢饮达旦，大醉，作此篇。兼怀子由。

míng yuè jǐ shí yǒu
明月几时有
bǎ jiǔ wèn qīng tiān
把酒问青天
bù zhī tiān shàng gōng què
不知天上宫阙
jīn xī shì hé nián
今夕是何年
wǒ yù chéng fēng guī qù
我欲乘风归去
yòu kǒng qióng lóu yù yǔ
又恐琼楼玉宇
gāo chù bù shèng hán
高处不胜寒
qǐ wǔ nòng qīng yǐng
起舞弄清影
hé shì zài rén jiān
何似在人间

II

Mid Autumn night of the year of Bing Chen, happy drinking till dawn. Utterly drunk, composed this for my brother Zi-You.

When did the bright moon come into being
I raise the wine cup to ask the sapphire sky
What year is tonight
in celestial palaces
I could ride the wind to return there
but fear the unbearable chill
high in jade towers with jeweled eaves
I dance with my crisp shadow
in delight known only to mortals

zhuǎn zhū gé

转朱阁

dī qǐ hù

低绮户

zhào wú mián

照无眠

bù yìng yǒu hèn

不应有恨

hé shì cháng xiàng bié shí yuán

何事长向别时圆

rén yǒu bēi huān lí hé

人有悲欢离合

yuè yǒu yīn qíng yuán quē

月有阴晴圆缺

cǐ shì gǔ nán quán

此事古难全

dàn yuàn rén cháng jiǔ

但愿人长久

qiān lǐ gòng chán juān

千里共婵娟

It rolls past crimson gates
casts through silk curtained windows
to light the sleepless
The moon has no regrets
Why does it fully glow over parted humans
Misery and joy cycle with each farewell and reunion
The moon wanes and waxes
Time forbids perfection
Let us live long to share moonlight's spell
though a thousand miles apart

三

欧阳文忠公尝问余，琴诗何者最善？答以退之听颍师琴诗最善。公曰，此诗最奇丽，然非听琴，乃听琵琶也。余深然之。建安章质夫家善琵琶者，乞为歌词。余久不作，特取退之词，稍加隐括，使就声律，以遗之云。

nì nì ér nǚ yǔ
昵昵儿女语
dēng huǒ yè wēi míng
灯火夜微明
ēn yuàn ěr rǔ lái qù
恩怨尔汝来去
tán zhǐ lèi hé shēng
弹指泪和声
hū biàn xuān'áng yǒng shì
忽变轩昂勇士
yī gǔ tián rán zuò qì
一鼓填然作气
qiān lǐ bù liú xíng
千里不留行
huí shǒu mù yún yuǎn
回首暮云远
fēi xù lǎn qīng míng
飞絮揽青冥

III

*Master Eu-Yang Xiu once asked me which among the guqin poems
is the finest. I replied that it is the poem composed by Han Tui-Zhi
after hearing Master Ying play the guqin. Master Eu-Yang said,
that poem is stunning in its beauty, but it describes not the impres-
sions of a guqin, but a pipa. I agree. Zhang Zhi-Fu has an expert
pipa player in his household in Jian An, who requested a tune poem
from me. I was unable to compose it for a long time. Eventually I
took Tui-Zhi's poem, revised it slightly to fit the tune, and gave it to
the pipa player.*

Murmurs ripple between boy and girl
An oil lamp barely punctures the night
The whispers of lovers ebb and flow
Fingers pluck sounds that stir tears
and suddenly morph into strapping warriors
Courage surges as a drum starts to thunder
The unstoppable gallop sweeps a thousand miles
Heads turn towards dusk clouds on the horizon
Willow fuzz dances in a sapphire sky

zhòng qín lǐ
众禽里
zhēn cǎi fèng
真彩凤
dú bù míng
独不鸣
jī pān cùn bù qiān xiǎn
跻攀寸步千险
yī luò bǎi xún qīng
一落百寻轻
fán zi zhǐ jiān fēng yǔ
烦子指间风雨
zhì wǒ cháng zhōng bīng tàn
置我肠中冰炭
qǐ zuò bù néng píng
起坐不能平
tuī shǒu cóng guī qù
推手从归去
wú lèi yǔ jūn qīng
无泪与君倾

Among the world's creatures
the iridescent phoenix alone
withholds its song
I climb a sheer cliff one inch at a time
then fall a thousand feet into an abyss
Your fingers conjure wind and rain
send ice and hot coal into my guts
When I can no longer sit still
you stop and leave
having exhausted my tears

nán xiāng zi

南乡子

一

chóng jiǔ hán huī lóu chéng xú jūn yóu
重九涵辉楼呈徐君猷

shuāng jiàng shuǐ hén shōu
霜降水痕收
qiǎn bì lín lín lù yuǎn zhōu
浅碧鳞鳞露远洲
jiǔ lì jiàn xiāo fēng lì ruǎn
酒力渐消风力软
sōu sōu
飕飕
pò mào duō qíng què liàn tóu
破帽多情却恋头

jiā jié ruò wèi chóu
佳节若为酬
dàn bǎ qīng zūn duàn sòng qiū
但把清樽断送秋
wàn shì dàotóu dōu shì mèng
万事到头都是梦
xiū xiū
休休
míng rì huáng huā dié yě chóu
明日黄花蝶也愁

To the Tune of "Southern Countryside"

I

For Xu Jun-You, on Hanhui Terrace on Double Ninth

Frost is on the ground and the river has shrunk
Distant shoals appear amid shimmering green shallows
As the wine wears off I begin to feel the wind
I shiver
My torn hat clings to my head with too many thoughts

How can I give thanks to autumn
Let me say goodbye with this sparkling cup
Everything becomes a dream in the end
Let this be enough
Tomorrow even butterflies will mourn the chrysanthemums

二

jí jù
集句

chàng wàng sòng chūn bēi
怅望送春杯
jiàn lǎo féng chūn néng jǐ huí
渐老逢春能几回
huā mǎn chǔ chéng chóu yuǎn bié
花满楚城愁远别
shāng huái
伤怀
hé kuàng qīng sī jí guǎn cuī
何况清丝急管催

yín duàn wàng xiāng tái
吟断望乡台
wàn lǐ guī xīn dú shàng lái
万里归心独上来
jǐng wù dēng lín xián shǐ jiàn
景物登临闲始见
pái huái
徘徊
yī cùn xiāng sī yī cùn huī
一寸相思一寸灰

II

Collected Lines

My gaze darkens the cup that sends off spring
How many more springs will I see as I age
Blossoms fill the ancient city as I mourn our separation
My memories sting
Whipped on by haunting strings and strident flutes

Sighs are exhausted on Gazing Homeward Terrace
My ache to return flares alone across thousands of
        miles
I have climbed to sights with eyes opened by forced
        leisure
Pace in circles
Each inch of yearning is followed by an inch of ashes

三

sòng shù gǔ
送述古

huí shǒu luàn shān héng
回首乱山横
bù jiàn jū rén zhǐ jiàn chéng
不见居人只见城
shéi shì lín píng shān shàng tǎ
谁似临平山上塔
tíng tíng
亭亭
yíng kè xī lái sòng kè xíng
迎客西来送客行

guī lù wǎn fēng qīng
归路晚风清
yī zhěn chū hán mèng bù chéng
一枕初寒梦不成
jīn yè cán dēng xié zhào chù
今夜残灯斜照处
yíng yíng
荧荧
qiū yǔ qíng shí lèi bù qíng
秋雨晴时泪不晴

III

Farewell to Shu-Gu

I looked back at the jumbled ridges
No sign of people only their walls
I envy the stupa on Linping Mountain
It stands tall
greeted travelers from the west and saw one off

Dusk wind swept over my path home
My pillow turns chill and dreams don't come
Tonight in the slanting light of a flickering lamp
tears glimmer
The autumn rains have stopped but not the tears

四

wǎn jǐng luò qióng bēi
晚景落琼杯

zhào yǎn yún shān cuì zuò duī
照眼云山翠作堆

rèn dé mín é chūn xuě làng
认得岷峨春雪浪

chū lái
初来

wàn qǐng pú táo zhǎng lù pēi
万顷蒲萄涨渌醅

chūn yǔ àn yáng tái
春雨暗阳台

luàn jiǔ gē lóu shī fěn sāi
乱酒歌楼湿粉腮

yī zhèn dōng fēng lái juǎn dì
一阵东风来卷地

chuī huí
吹回

luò zhào jiāng tiān yī bàn kāi
落照江天一半开

IV

A jade goblet captures late afternoon landscape
Mountains glisten through clouds in layers of green
I recognize spring snow from lofty Min and Emei
Just melted
Ten thousand acres of grapes churn into wine

Spring rain darkens the balcony
Disturbs wine and song and wets powdered cheeks
A burst of east wind sweeps through the land
Blows back
Opens half sky half river to evening glow

dìng fēng bō
定风波

一

三月七日，沙湖道中遇雨。雨具先去，同行皆狼狈，余独不觉。已而遂晴，故作此词。

mò tīng chuān lín dǎ yè shēng
莫听穿林打叶声
hé fáng yín xiào qiě xú xíng
何妨吟啸且徐行
zhú zhàng máng xié qīng shèng mǎ
竹杖芒鞋轻胜马
shéi pà
谁怕
yī suō yān yǔ rèn píng shēng
一蓑烟雨任平生

liào qiào chūn fēng chuī jiǔ xǐng
料峭春风吹酒醒
wēi lěng
微冷
shān tóu xié zhào què xiāng yíng
山头斜照却相迎
huí shǒu xiàng lái xiāo sǎ chù
回首向来潇洒处
guī qù
归去
yě wú fēng yǔ yě wú qíng
也无风雨也无晴

To the Tune of "Calming the Wind and Waves"

I

On the seventh day of the Third Month, it rained on our way to Sandy Lake. We had sent the rain gear ahead of us. Everyone was embarrassed by the soak, except for me. Soon it cleared, and I composed this.

Ignore the sounds piercing trees and beating leaves
Why not chant a little or sing and take our time
Bamboo staff and straw sandals   lighter than riding
    a horse
What could I fear
A capeful of fog and rain all my life

The rush of spring wind blows away all traces of wine
A little cold
Up on the mountain slant light beams greet us
Look back toward where the storm raged
We could return
It is neither rainy nor clear

二

cháng xiàn rén jiān zuó yù láng
常羡人间琢玉郎
tiān jiào fēn fù diǎn sū niáng
天教分付点酥娘
zì zuò qīng gē chuán hào chǐ
自作清歌传皓齿
fēng qǐ
风起
xuě fēi yán hǎi biàn qīng liáng
雪飞炎海变清凉

wàn lǐ guī lái nián yù shào
万里归来年愈少
wēi xiào
微笑
xiào shí yóu dài lǐng méi xiāng
笑时犹带岭梅香
shì wèn lǐng nán yīng bù hǎo
试问岭南应不好
què dào
却道
cǐ xīn'ān chù shì wú xiāng
此心安处是吾乡

II

I envy a certain man refined as carved jade
destined to match with a consummate artist
Singing her composition she reveals the whitest teeth
The wind rises
Snowflakes cool an ocean of flames

Looking even younger returning from a distant journey
she smiles
spreading the perfume of Plum Blossom Ridge
I ask about the hard life south of the Ridges
and she says
wherever my heart settles I'm home

mǎn tíng fāng
满庭芳

一

有王长官者，弃官黄州三十三年，黄人谓之王先生。因送陈
慥来过余，因为赋此。

sān shí sān nián
三十三年
jīn shéi cún zhě
今谁存者
suàn zhǐ jūn yǔ cháng jiāng
算只君与长江
lǐn rán cāng guì
凛然苍桧
shuāng gàn kǔ nán shuāng
霜干苦难双
wén dào sī zhōu gǔ xiàn
闻道司州古县
yún xī shàng
云溪上
zhú wù sōng chuāng
竹坞松窗
jiāng nán àn
江南岸
bù yīn sòng zi
不因送子
nìng kěn guò wú bāng
宁肯过吾邦

To the Tune of
"The Court Fills with Fragrance"

I

There was a Governor Wang, who abandoned the office of Huang-zhou for thirty three years. The people of Huangzhou called him Master Wang. He accompanied my friend Chen Zao to see him off. They passed Huangzhou and visited with me. I composed this poem in his honor.

After thirty-three years
who still matters
I count only you and the Yangtze River
A towering juniper in cool green
Its frosted trunk unmatched in endurance
I hear that in a nearby ancient county
by streams mirroring clouds
your pine windows open from bamboo walls
On the Yangtze's south shore
only to see off a friend
you stop by my humble home

chuāng chuāng
摐摐
shū yǔ guò
疏雨过
fēng lín wǔ pò
风林舞破
yān gài yún chuáng
烟盖云幢
yuàn chí cǐ yāo jūn
愿持此邀君
yī yǐn kōng gāng
一饮空缸
jū shì xiān shēng lǎo yǐ
居士先生老矣
zhēn mèng lǐ xiāng duì cán gāng
真梦里相对残釭
gē shēng duàn
歌声断
xíng rén wèi qǐ
行人未起
chuán gǔ yǐ féng féng
船鼓已逢逢

Raindrops patter
Sparse and brief
The forest breaks into a wind dance
beneath smoke canopies and cloud banners
With this cup I invite you
to drink till the jar is empty
Both you and I have aged
facing a sputtering lamp in a dream
The singing stops
The traveler does not rise
The boatmen have begun to drum

二

wō jiǎo xū míng
蜗角虚名
yíng tóu wēi lì
蝇头微利
suàn lái zhuó shén gān máng
算来着甚干忙
shì jiē qián dìng
事皆前定
shéi ruò yòu shéi qiáng
谁弱又谁强
qiě chèn xián shēn wèi lǎo
且趁闲身未老
xū fàng wǒ
须放我
xiē zi shū kuáng
些子疏狂
bǎi nián lǐ
百年里
hún jiào shì zuì
浑教是醉
sān wàn liù qiān cháng
三万六千场

II

Fame fits in a snail's horn
Profit balances a fly's head
No calculation justifies the toil
Destiny tracks us all
The weak along with the strong
Unemployed and not yet old
I allow myself
to go a little wild
For one hundred years
let me get drunk
thirty six thousand times

sī liàng
思量
néng jǐxǔ
能几许
yōu chóu fēng yǔ
忧愁风雨
yī bàn xiāng fáng
一半相妨
yòu hé xū dǐ sǐ
又何须抵死
shuō duǎn lùn cháng
说短论长
xìng duì qīng fēng hào yuè
幸对清风皓月
tái yīn zhǎn
苔茵展
yún mù gāo zhāng
云幕高张
jiāng nán hǎo
江南好
qiān zhōng měi jiǔ
千钟美酒
yī qǔ mǎn tíng fāng
一曲满庭芳

Consider the length
of our existence
The wind-tangled rain of sorrow
erodes half of it
Why invite death with endless
arguing over the short and the long
In luck we face crystal wind and lustrous moon
on a carpet of soft moss
Clouds weave a towering tent
South of the Yangtze enchants
with a thousand goblets of divine wine
to the tune of "The Court Fills with Fragrance"

三

元丰七年四月一日，余将去黄移汝，留别雪堂邻里二三君子，会李仲览自江东来别，遂书以遗之。

guī qù lái xī
归去来兮
wú guī hé chù
吾归何处
wàn lǐ jiā zài mín é
万里家在岷峨
bǎi nián qiáng bàn
百年强半
lái rì kǔ wú duō
来日苦无多
zuò jiàn huáng zhōu zài rùn
坐见黄州再闰
ér tóng jìn
儿童尽
chǔ yǔ wú gē
楚语吴歌
shān zhōng yǒu
山中友
jī tún shè jiǔ
鸡豚社酒
xiāng quàn lǎo dōng pō
相劝老东坡

III

*On the first day of the Fourth Month, seventh year of Yuan Feng, I
was about to leave Huangzhou for Ruzhou. A few gentlemen from
the Snow Hall neighborhood gathered to say goodbye. From the
east of the Yangtze River, Li Zhong-Lan came. I composed this in
his honor.*

"Return to where I belong"
Where do I belong
Home near Min and Emei thousands of miles away
My hundred years nearly half gone
The coming days won't be many
Suddenly I've seen another leap year in Huangzhou
All of my children
speak and sing in the local dialect
Friends from these mountains
with chicken and pork and festival wine
urge me to grow old at East Hill

yún hé
云何

dāng cǐ qù
当此去

rén shēng dǐ shì
人生底事

lái wǎng rú suō
来往如梭

dài xián kàn qiū fēng
待闲看秋风

luò shuǐ qīng bō
洛水清波

hǎo zài táng qián xì liǔ
好在堂前细柳

yīng niàn wǒ
应念我

mò jiǎn róu kē
莫剪柔柯

réng chuán yǔ
仍传语

jiāng nán fù lǎo
江南父老

shí yǔ shài yú suō
时与晒渔蓑

What can I say
as I leave here
the events of our lives
come and go like a shuttle
I'll soon be watching the autumn wind
stir crystal waves of the Luo
Lucky for these slender willows by my house
Thinking of me
no one will lop their tender branches
Pass the word
to elders along the Yangtze
sun my fishing cape now and then

huàn xī shā

浣溪沙

一

xú zhōu shí tán xiè yǔ
徐州石潭谢雨

zhào rì shēn hóng nuǎn jiàn yú
照日深红暖见鱼
lián cūn lǜ àn wǎn cáng wū
连村绿暗晚藏乌
huáng tóng bái sǒu jù suī xū
黄童白叟聚睢盱

mí lù féng rén suī wèi guàn
麋鹿逢人虽未惯
yuán náo wén gǔ bù xū hū
猿猱闻鼓不须呼
guī lái shuō yǔ cǎi sāng gū
归来说与采桑姑

To the Tune of "Sand of the Washing Stream"

I

Giving Thanks After Rain at Stone Pond in Xuzhou

Crimson warmth of sunset lured fish to the surface
Villages joined at dusk with crow-hiding woods
Toddlers and old men flocked to the show in wide-eyed
    delight

Deer shied at the sight of the visiting governor
Monkeys heard drums and required no invitation
All told to mulberry-leaf picking women when they
    returned

二

游蕲水清泉寺，寺临兰溪，溪水西流。

shān xià lán yá duǎn jìn xī
山下兰芽短浸溪
sōng jiān shā lù jìng wú ní
松间沙路净无泥
xiāo xiāo mù yǔ zǐ guī tí
萧萧暮雨子规啼

shéi dào rén shēng wú zài shào
谁道人生无再少
mén qián liú shuǐ shàng néng xī
门前流水尚能西
xiū jiāng bái fà chàng huáng jī
休将白发唱黄鸡

II

*I visited Crystal Spring Temple in Qishui County. The temple over-
looks a stream lined by orchids. The stream flows westward.*

The stream bathes orchid sprouts down the mountain
No mud stains the sandy path among pines
A cuckoo cries out as the dusk rain patters

Who says life does not bloom in youth again
Even the water at my doorstep can flow west
Do not mourn white hair and sing of the golden rooster

三

xuán mǒ hóng zhuāng kàn shǐ jūn
旋抹红妆看使君
sān sān wǔ wǔ jí lí mén
三三五五棘篱门
xiāng pái tà pò qiàn luó qún
相排踏破茜罗裙

lǎo yòu fú xié shōu mài shè
老幼扶携收麦社
wū yuān xiáng wǔ sài shén cūn
乌鸢翔舞赛神村
dào féng zuì sǒu wò huáng hūn
道逢醉叟卧黄昏

III

They rouged in a whirl to go governor watching
gathered in threes and fives by the date hedge gates
pushed each other and trampled on vermilion silk skirts

The young led the old to the wheat harvest ritual
Crows and hawks danced in circles above the village
    shrine
By the road an old drunk lay down in the sunset

四

wàn qǐng fēng tāo bù jì sū
万顷风涛不记苏
xuě qíng jiāng shàng mài qiān chē
雪晴江上麦千车
dàn lìng rén bǎo wǒ chóu wú
但令人饱我愁无

cuì xiù yǐ fēng yíng liǔ xù
翠袖倚风萦柳絮
jiàng chún dé jiǔ làn yīng zhū
绛唇得酒烂樱珠
zūn qián hē shǒu niè shuāng xū
樽前呵手镊霜须

IV

Ten thousand acres of wintry waves erased my memory
Riverside snow glistens foretelling a thousand wagons
    of wheat
No gloom haunts me when no one goes hungry

A courtesan's jade sleeves dance in the wind with
    catkins of snow
Her crimson lips sip wine to become a pearl of ripe
    cherry
Goblet down I warm hands over my breath and hold my
    frosted beard

五

ruǎn cǎo píng shā guò yǔ xīn
软草平莎过雨新
qīng shā zǒu mǎ lù wú chén
轻沙走马路无尘
hé shí shōu shí ǒu gēng shēn
何时收拾耦耕身

rì nuǎn sāng má guāng shì pō
日暖桑麻光似泼
fēng lái hāo ài qì rú xūn
风来蒿艾气如薰
shǐ jūn yuán shì qí zhōng rén
使君元是其中人

V

Soft grass and flat sedge freshen after rain
My horse trots on a sandy road free of dust
When will I pack up to plow side by side with a friend?

Mulberry trees and hemp warm in pools of sunlight
Mugworts exhale scent of vanilla into the wind
I   the governor   finally in my element

六

sù sù yī jīn luò zǎo huā
簌簌衣巾落枣花
cūn nán cūn běi xiǎng sāo chē
村南村北响缲车
niú yī gǔ liǔ mài huáng guā
牛衣古柳卖黄瓜

jiǔ kùn lù cháng wéi yù shuì
酒困路长惟欲睡
rì gāo rén kě màn sī chá
日高人渴漫思茶
qiāo mén shì wèn yě rén jiā
敲门试问野人家

VI

Date blossoms rain onto my clothes
Loud spindles reel silk from village south to north
A hemp-clad man sells cucumbers by an ancient willow

Tired by wine and a long journey I desire sleep
thirst for tea as the sun climbs high
knock on the door of a rustic house to try my luck

七

fēng yā qīng yún tiē shuǐ fēi
风压轻云贴水飞
zhà qíng chí guǎn yàn zhēng ní
乍晴池馆燕争泥
shěn láng duō bìng bù shèng yī
沈郎多病不胜衣

shā shàng bù wén hóng yàn xìn
沙上不闻鸿雁信
zhú jiān shí tīng zhè gū tí
竹间时听鹧鸪啼
cǐ qíng wéi yǒu luò huā zhī
此情惟有落花知

VII

The wind flies fast clouds low over the water
The sky clears over swallows nesting at pond-side lodge
Burdened with illness Lord Shen could barely dress

No sound of letter-bearing wild geese over the sand
Occasional cries of partridges among bamboos
Only fallen blossoms know my sentiments

江城子

一

乙卯正月二十日记梦

shí nián shēng sǐ liǎng máng máng
十年生死两茫茫
bù sī liàng
不思量
zì nán wàng
自难忘
qiān lǐ gū fén
千里孤坟
wú chù huà qī liáng
无处话凄凉
zòng shǐ xiāng féng yīng bù shí
纵使相逢应不识
chén mǎn miàn
尘满面
bìn rú shuāng
鬓如霜

To the Tune of
"From the River City"

I

A Dream on the Twentieth of the First Month

Ten years one alive one dead we share no light
I do not dwell on it
can never forget
A thousand miles away a lonely tomb
I could tell no one about my sorrow
Even if we should meet you would not recognize me
Dust covers my face
On my temples hair white as frost

yè lái yōu mèng hū huán xiāng
夜来幽梦忽还乡
xiǎo xuān chuāng
小轩窗
zhèng shū zhuāng
正梳妆
xiāng gù wú yán
相顾无言
wéi yǒu lèi qiān háng
惟有泪千行
liào dé nián nián cháng duàn chù
料得年年肠断处
míng yuè yè
明月夜
duǎn sōng gāng
短松岗

Last night a serene dream took me home
Facing the little window
you combed your long hair
Gazing at each other we were wordless
Only tears fell in a thousand lines
I know that each year grief shall twist your innards
on a moon-infused night
in your mound beneath short pines

二

gū shān zhú gé sòng shù gǔ
孤山竹阁送述古

cuì é xiū dài qiè rén kàn
翠蛾羞黛怯人看
yǎn shuāng wán
掩霜纨
lèi tōu tán
泪偷弹
qiě jìn yī zūn
且尽一尊
shōu lèi chàng yáng guān
收泪唱阳关
màn dào dì chéng tiān yàng yuǎn
漫道帝城天样远
tiān yì jiàn
天易见
jiàn jūn nán
见君难

II

Composed for a courtesan, to be sung to Shu-Gu in the Bamboo
Pavilion of the Lone Mountain Temple.

Afraid of being seen beneath my darkened eyebrows
I cover my face with a frost-white silk fan
shed tears in stealth
Time to drain the chalice
hold back tears and sing *The Sun Pass*
People say the imperial city is far as the sky
Easy to see the sky
but not you

huà táng xīn gòu jìn gū shān
画堂新构近孤山
qū lán gàn
曲栏干
wèi shéi ān
为谁安
fēi xù luò huā
飞絮落花
chūn sè shǔ míng nián
春色属明年
yù zhào xiǎo zhōu xún jiù shì
欲棹小舟寻旧事
wú chù wèn
无处问
shuǐ lián tiān
水连天

An ornate hall stands new on Lone Mountain
Undulating railings
installed for whom?
Catkins fly into falling flowers
Spring will return next year
I will row a little boat to trace memories
with no one to help me
Water will blend with the sky

三

hèn bié xú zhōu
恨别徐州

tiān yá liú luò sī wú qióng
天涯流落思无穷
jì xiāng féng
既相逢
què cōng cōng
却匆匆
xié shǒu jiā rén
携手佳人
hé lèi zhé cán hóng
和泪折残红
wèi wèn dōng fēng yú jǐ xǔ
为问东风余几许
chūn zòng zài
春纵在
yǔ shéi tóng
与谁同

III

Farewell at Xuzhou

Inflicted with endless pining I drift to the edge of the
    sky
We were destined to meet
in such haste
Hand in hand with a beauty
with tears I plucked withering plum blossoms
How much east wind is left?
Spring gleams
No one to share it with

suí dī sān yuè shuǐ róng róng
隋堤三月水溶溶

bèi guī hóng
背归鸿

qù wú zhōng
去吴中

huí shǒu péng chéng
回首彭城

qīng sì yǔ huái tōng
清泗与淮通

jì wǒ xiāng sī qiān diǎn lèi
寄我相思千点泪

liú bù dào
流不到

chǔ jiāng dōng
楚江东

April water rose against Sui Dynasty embankments
Against homing geese
I departed south for Wuzhong
My head turns back toward Xuzhou
Water glistens a return path
I post a thousand teardrops of longing
to reach you
River Chu intercepts them east

四

mèng zhōng liǎo liǎo zuì zhōng xǐng
梦中了了醉中醒
zhǐ yuān míng
只渊明
shì qián shēng
是前生
zǒu biàn rén jiān
走遍人间
yī jiù què gōng gēng
依旧却躬耕
zuó yè dōng pō chūn yǔ zú
昨夜东坡春雨足
wū què xǐ
乌鹊喜
bào xīn qíng
报新晴

IV

I saw it all and woke from the drunken dream
The poet Yuan Ming was
myself in a previous life
Trudged far and wide in mortals' world
Bent over a plough in the end
Last night spring rain drenched East Hill
Crows delight to report
a clear fresh sky

xuě táng xī pàn àn quán míng
雪堂西畔暗泉鸣
běi shān qīng
北山倾
xiǎo xī héng
小溪横
nán wàng tíng qiū
南望亭丘
gū xiù sǒng zēng chéng
孤秀耸曾城
dōu shì xié chuān dāng rì jǐng
都是斜川当日景
wú lǎo yě
吾老也
jì yú líng
寄馀龄

A hidden spring sings westward of Snow Hall
Mountains lean in from the north
A slender stream crosses my path
The pavilion on a southerly hill evokes
a lone beauty towering above a storied peak
Scenes as recorded by Yuan-Ming in Slant Valley
I am old enough to entrust to these
the remainder of my days

五

湖上与张先同赋，时闻弹筝。

fèng huáng shān xià yǔ chū qíng
凤凰山下雨初晴
shuǐ fēng qīng
水风清
wǎn xiá míng
晚霞明
yī duǒ fú qú
一朵芙蕖
kāi guò shàng yíng yíng
开过尚盈盈
hé chù fēi lái shuāng bái lù
何处飞来双白鹭
rú yǒu yì
如有意
mù pīng tíng
慕娉婷

V

Composed on the West Lake along with Zhang Xian's poem, when we heard a woman pluck strings of zheng in another boat.

The rain clears by the Phoenix Mountain
The wind combs the water
Sunset clouds glow
A long stem of lotus flower
poises on the cusp of withering
A pair of white herons descend from nowhere
Entranced
they gaze upon the voluptuous bloom

hū wén jiāng shàng nòng āi zhēng
忽闻江上弄哀筝

kǔ hán qíng
苦含情

qiǎn shéi tīng
遣谁听

yān liǎn yún shōu
烟敛云收

yī yuē shì xiāng líng
依约是湘灵

yù dài qǔ zhōng xún wèn qǔ
欲待曲终寻问取

rén bù jiàn
人不见

shù fēng qīng
数峰青

Suddenly string sounds wash over the lake
Sadness braids with entreaty
Unbearable to hear
The mist falls and clouds fade
Hushed by the Xiang Princesses' drowned beauty
We seek the musician when the tune ends
No sign of her
Green peaks freeze in flight

六

mì zhōu chū liè

密州出猎

lǎo fū liáo fā shào nián kuáng

老夫聊发少年狂

zuǒ qiān huáng

左牵黄

yòu qíng cāng

右擎苍

jǐn mào diāo qiú

锦帽貂裘

qiān qí juǎn píng gāng

千骑卷平冈

wèi bào qīng chéng suí tài shǒu

为报倾城随太守

qīn shè hǔ

亲射虎

kàn sūn láng

看孙郎

VI

Hunt in Mizhou

An old man lets loose some youthful wildness
Left hand leads the yellow dog
Right shoulder holds the gray eagle
Satin hat and marten cloak
A thousand horses sweep across the plateau
Since the entire city has followed its governor
he shall shoot the tiger himself
just like Lord Sun

jiǔ hān xiōng dǎn shàng kāi zhāng

酒酣胸胆尚开张

bìn wēi shuāng

鬓微霜

yòu hé fáng

又何妨

chí jié yún zhōng

持节云中

hé rì qiǎn féng táng

何日遣冯唐

huì wǎn diāo gōng rú mǎn yuè

会挽雕弓如满月

xī běi wàng

西北望

shè tiān láng

射天狼

Given enough wine my spirits soar
My hair a trifle frosted on the temples
What harm could it be
I can hold the border against barbarians
When will the court send marching orders
I can pull my carved bow into a full moon
look northwest
to bring down the Sky Wolf

dòng xiān gē

洞仙歌

余七岁时, 见眉山老尼姓朱, 忘其名, 年九十余, 自言: 尝随其师入蜀主孟昶宫中. 一日大热, 蜀主与花蕊夫人夜起避暑摩诃池上, 作一词. 朱具能记之. 今四十年, 朱已死, 人无知此词者. 但记其首两句, 暇日寻味, 岂洞仙歌令乎, 乃为足之.

bīng jī yù gǔ
冰肌玉骨
zì qīng liáng wú hàn
自清凉无汗
shuǐ diàn fēng lái àn xiāng mǎn
水殿风来暗香满
xiù lián kāi
绣帘开
yī diǎn míng yuè kuī rén
一点明月窥人
rén wèi qǐn
人未寝
yī zhěn chāi héng bìn luàn
欹枕钗横鬓乱

To the Tune of "The Song of the Cave Celestial"

At age seven, I met an old nun from Meishan. Her last name was Zhu, I have forgotten her first name. She was past ninety, said she once followed her master into the palace household of King Meng Chang of Shu. One day, the heat was overwhelming, the King and Lady Hua Rui rose during the night to seek the cool night air by the Mojie Pond. Zhu could still remember the poem the King composed that night. It has been forty years; Zhu is long dead. No one alive knows that poem. I can only remember the first two lines. I pondered these in my spare time. Would they not fit the tune of "Song of the Cave Celestial"? Here they are, I added the rest.

Skin of ice and bones of jade
By nature free of sweat
The wind floods the Water Pavilion with deep fragrance
Embroidered curtains part
A sliver of bright moon peeks in
You are still not sleeping
Leaning on the pillow with gold pins loose and your
    hair down

qǐ lái xié sù shǒu
起来携素手
tíng hù wú shēng
庭户无声
shí jiàn shū xīng dù hé hàn
时见疏星渡河汉
shì wèn yè rúhé
试问夜如何
yè yǐ sān gēng
夜已三更
jīn bō dàn
金波淡
yù shéng dī zhuǎn
玉绳低转
dàn qū zhǐ
但屈指
xī fēng jǐshí lái
西风几时来
yòu bù dào
又不道
liú nián àn zhōng tōu huàn
流年暗中偷换

You rise and I take your white hand
Not a sound within the palace
Now and then a star crosses the Celestial River
You ask how is the night?
The night is already past three
Moonlight grows faint
The Jade String has set
I reckon with my fingers
when is the west wind due
Needless to say
the years sneak past in unseen flow

bā shēng gān zhōu
八声甘州

jì cān liáo zi
寄参寥子

yǒu qíng fēng wàn lǐ juǎn cháo lái
有情风万里卷潮来
wú qíng sòng cháo guī
无情送潮归
wèn qián táng jiāng shàng
问钱塘江上
xī xīng pǔ kǒu
西兴浦口
jǐ dù xié huī
几度斜晖
bù yòng sī liáng jīn gǔ
不用思量今古
fǔ yǎng xī rén fēi
俯仰昔人非
shéi shì dōng pō lǎo
谁似东坡老
bái shǒu wàng jī
白首忘机

To the Tune of "Eight Toned Ganzhou"

A Letter to Can Liao Zi

Passionate wind sweeps tides in for a thousand miles
sees tides off with indifference
Along the Qiantang River
at the Xixing Beach
how many times we watched sunsets
No use judging past and present as heroes perished
in the time it takes to throw back one's head
Who is like old Dong-Po
white haired and free of schemes

jì qǔ xī hú xī pàn
记取西湖西畔
zhèng chūn shān hǎo chù
正春山好处
kōng cuì yān fēi
空翠烟霏
suàn shī rén xiāng dé
算诗人相得
rú wǒ yǔ jūn xī
如我与君稀
yuē tā nián
约他年
dōng huán hǎi dào
东还海道
yuàn xiè gōng yǎ zhì mò xiāng wéi
愿谢公雅志莫相违
xī zhōu lù
西州路
bù yīng huí shǒu
不应回首
wèi wǒ zhān yī
为我沾衣

Remember west shore of West Lake
A mountain in the perfection of spring
Airy green in shifting mist
Among poets who harmonize
few are as close as we
Let us plan to return east someday
follow the Yangtze river toward the sea
Let me not die in regret like Lord Xie
When you pass Yangzhou's West Gate
you shall not turn back your head
and stain your sleeve with tears for me

bǔ suàn zi

卜算子

黄州定慧院寓居作

què yuè guà shū tóng
缺月挂疏桐
lòu duàn rén chū jìng
漏断人初静
shéi jiàn yōu rén dú wǎng lái
谁见幽人独往来
piāo miǎo gū hóng yǐng
缥缈孤鸿影

jīng qǐ què huí tóu
惊起却回头
yǒu hèn wú rén xǐng
有恨无人省
jiǎn jìn hán zhī bù kěn qī
拣尽寒枝不肯栖
jì mò shā zhōu lěng
寂寞沙洲冷

To the Tune of
"Divination"

Composed at my home Ding Hui Yuan in Huangzhou.

A broken moon catches on a leafless phoenix tree
The water-clock stops dripping in the budding quiet
No one sees the pensive one drift alone
A solitary swan veiled by darkness

Startled she flees yet turns back her head
No one knows her regrets
Picking through chill branches she would not perch
Cold binds her to the deserted sand isle

点绛唇
diǎn jiàng chún

红杏飘香
hóng xìng piāo xiāng
柳含烟翠拖轻缕
liǔ hán yān cuì tuō qīng lǚ
水边朱户
shuǐ biān zhū hù
尽卷黄昏雨
jìn juǎn huáng hūn yǔ

烛影摇风
zhú yǐng yáo fēng
一枕伤春绪
yī zhěn shāng chūn xù
归不去
guī bù qù
凤楼何处
fèng lóu hé chù
芳草迷归路
fāng cǎo mí guī lù

To the Tune of "Touching Up Crimson Lips"

Red apricot blossoms flaunt sweet scent
Willows trail deft strands of wispy green
On the shore at the vermillion window
She rolls up the curtain only to see dusk rain

The candle's shadow traces the wind
My pillow fills with spring sadness
I can't find my way back
Phoenix Mansion beckons
Fragrant grass obscures the path

ruǎn láng guī
阮郎归

chūxià
初夏

lù huái gāo liǔ yè xīn chán
绿槐高柳咽新蝉
xūn fēng chū rù xián
熏风初入弦
bì shā chuāng xià shuǐ chén yān
碧纱窗下水沉烟
qí shēng jīng zhòu mián
棋声惊昼眠

wēi yǔ guò
微雨过
xiǎo hé fān
小荷翻
liú huā kāi yù rán
榴花开欲燃
yù pén xiān shǒu nòng qīng quán
玉盆纤手弄清泉
qióng zhū suì què yuán
琼珠碎却圆

To the Tune of "Lord Ruan's Return"

Early Summer

First cicadas drone in leafy locusts and tall willows
Summer Wind is heard again on strings
Incense smoke dances below green window-gauze
The sound of chess interrupts a nap

A light rain passes
flips tiny lotus leaves
Pomegranate flowers are about to burst into flames
Slender hands tease the crystal spring with a jade basin
Pearls shatter then become round again

shào nián yóu
少年游

润州作、代人寄远.

qù nián xiāng sòng
去年相送
yú háng mén wài
余杭门外
fēi xuě shì yáng huā
飞雪似杨花
jīn nián chūn jìn
今年春尽
yáng huā sì xuě
杨花似雪
yóu bù jiàn huán jiā
犹不见还家

duì jiǔ juǎn lián yāo míng yuè
对酒卷帘邀明月
fēng lù tòu chuāng shā
风露透窗纱
qià sì héng é lián shuāng yàn
恰似姮娥怜双燕
fēn míng zhào
分明照
huà liáng xié
画梁斜

To the Tune of
"A Young Man's Journey"

Composed in Runzhou, to send afar for someone.

Last year I saw you off
beyond the Yuhang Gate
Snowflakes danced like willow fuzz
This year at the end of spring
willow catkins unleash their snow
You still have not come home

I roll up the curtains and invite the moon to wine
Windblown dew seeps through the window screen
The moon goddess favors a pair of swallows
lights up their nest in full
on the lotus painted roof beam

归朝欢

和苏坚伯固

wǒ mèng piān zhōu fú zhèn zé
我梦扁舟浮震泽
xuě làng yáo kōng qiān qǐng bái
雪浪摇空千顷白
jué lái mǎn yǎn shì lú shān
觉来满眼是庐山
yǐ tiān wú shù kāi qīng bì
倚天无数开青壁
cǐ shēng zhǎng jiē xī
此生长接浙
yǔ jūn tóng shì jiāng nán kè
与君同是江南客
mèng zhōng yóu
梦中游
jué lái qīng shǎng
觉来清赏
tóng zuò fēi suō zhì
同作飞梭掷

To the Tune of
"The Joy of Returning to Court"

In Reply to Su Bo-Gu

I dreamed I was in a little boat floating on Thunder
    Lake
Snowy waves thrashed a thousand acres white
When I awoke Mount Lu filled my eyes
Countless green cliffs rising into the sky
I often gather up wet rice and run
You and I both travelers south of the Yangtze
We journey in a dream
wake to this pure pleasure
then fly as shuttles across a loom

míng rì xī fēng hái guà xí
明日西风还挂席
chàng wǒ xīn cí lèi zhān yì
唱我新词泪沾臆
líng jūn qù hòu chǔ shān kōng
灵均去后楚山空
lǐ yáng lán zhǐ wú yán sè
澧阳兰芷无颜色
jūn cái rú mèng dé
君才如梦得
wǔ líng gèng zài xī nán jí
武陵更在西南极
zhú zhī cí
竹枝词
mò yáo xīn chàng
莫徭新唱
shéi wèi gǔ jīn gé
谁谓古今隔

Tomorrow you shall sail off into the west wind
singing my new poem as tears stain your robe
Qu Yuan's passing made Chu Mountains empty
Orchids in Liyang have lost their colors
Your talents recall Liu Yu-Xi
sent to Wuling in the far Southwest
He composed Bamboo Tunes for the Yao
who shall also sing your new poems
Poetry bridges past and present

贺新郎

夏景

rǔ yàn fēi huá wū

乳燕飞华屋

qiǎo wú rén

悄无人

tóng yīn zhuǎn wǔ

桐阴转午

wǎn liáng xīn yù

晚凉新浴

shǒu nòng shēng xiāo bái tuán shàn

手弄生绡白团扇

shàn shǒu yī shí sì yù

扇手一时似玉

jiàn kùn yǐ

渐困倚

gū mián qīng shú

孤眠清熟

lián wài shéi lái tuī xiù hù

帘外谁来推绣户

wǎng jiào rén mèng duàn yáo tái qǔ

枉教人梦断瑶台曲

yòu què shì

又却是

fēng qiāo zhú

风敲竹

To the Tune of
"To the Bridegroom"

Summer

A fledging swallow flies into the mansion
quiet and deserted
The phoenix trees' shade transforms the day
Rising from a bath in the evening cool
I wave a round fan of white silk
The fan and my hand both resemble jade
Growing tired I recline
fall alone into a serene slumber
Who pushes the carved door beyond the curtains?
It shatters in vain a dream of singing on celestial
    terraces
It is only the wind
knocking on bamboos

shí liú bàn tǔ hóng jīn cù
石榴半吐红巾蹙

dài fú huā
待浮花

làng ruǐ dōu jìn
浪蕊都尽

bàn jūn yōu dú
伴君幽独

nóng yàn yī zhī xì kàn qǔ
秾艳一枝细看取

fāng xīn qiān chóng shì shù
芳心千重似束

yòu kǒng bèi
又恐被

qiū fēng jīng lù
秋风惊绿

ruò dài dé jūn lái xiàng cǐ
若待得君来向此

huā qián duì jiǔ bù rěn chù
花前对酒不忍触

gòng fěn lèi
共粉泪

liǎng sù sù
两簌簌

Half open pomegranate flowers reveal folded red
    scarves
Once the shallow blossoms'
flirtatious filaments are gone
they accompany you in solitude
Study a stem in its full glory
A thousand folds of sweet petals tightly bound
What happens when
the autumn wind startles green leaves
If you return then
can you drink wine and bear to touch the flower
Together with my rouged tears
the petals shall rain down

jiǎn zì mù lán huā

减字木兰花

钱塘西湖有诗僧清顺，所居藏春坞，门前有二古松，各有凌霄花络其上，顺常昼卧其下。余为郡，一日屏骑从过之，松风骚然，顺指落花求韵，余为赋之。

shuāng lóng duì qǐ
双龙对起
bái jiǎ cāng rán yān yǔ lǐ
白甲苍髯烟雨里
shū yǐng wēi xiāng
疏影微香
xià yǒu yōu rén zhòu mèng cháng
下有幽人昼梦长

hú fēng qīng ruǎn
湖风轻软
shuāng què fēi lái zhēng zào wǎn
双鹊飞来争噪晚
cuì zhǎn hóng qīng
翠飐红轻
shí xià líng xiāo bǎi chǐ yīng
时下凌霄百尺英

To the Tune of "Trimmed Magnolia"

By the West Lake in Hangzhou, there was a poet monk, Qing Shun, who resided at the Hidden Spring Cove. Before his door were two ancient pines, each entangled by trumpet vine. Shun often lay down beneath them in daylight. When I was the local governor, I passed by one day without my horse-riding entourage. Pine wind blew, Shun pointed to fallen flowers and asked for a poem. I composed this.

A pair of dragons rise face to face
white-scaled and blue-bearded in misty rain
Faint fragrance and scattered shadows
fall upon a daydreaming recluse

On a soft wind from the lake
two magpies arrive and argue till night
From viridian branches and airy vermilion
a trumpet blossom tumbles a hundred feet

lín jiāng xiān

临江仙

一

sòng qián mù fù

送钱穆父

yī bié dū mén sān gǎi huǒ
一别都门三改火
tiān yá tà jìn hóng chén
天涯踏尽红尘
yī rán yīxiào zuò chūn wēn
依然一笑作春温
wú bō zhēn gǔ jǐng
无波真古井
yǒu jié shì qiū yún
有节是秋筠

chóu chàng gū fān lián yè fā
惆怅孤帆连夜发
sòng xíng dàn yuè wēi yún
送行淡月微云
zūn qián bù yòng cuì méi pín
尊前不用翠眉颦
rén shēng rú nì lǚ
人生如逆旅
wǒ yě shì xíng rén
我也是行人

To the Tune of
"The Celestial by the River"

I

Farewell to Qian Mu-Fu

We've rekindled the hearth three times since parting
From the capital's gate trod world's dust to sky's edge
We smile at each other still and it's warm as spring
No waves stir the most ancient of wells
Bamboos stand tall in autumn wind

A solitary sail will depart into the sullen night
The pale moon and little clouds will see you off
Courtesans need not knit their brows as we drink
Life is but a guesthouse
I am your fellow traveler

二

龙丘子自洛之蜀，载二侍女，戎装骏马。至溪山佳处，辄留。见者以为异人。后十年，筑室黄冈之北，号静安居士。作此记之。

xì mǎ yuǎn tuó shuāng shì nǚ
细马远驮双侍女
qīng jīn yù dài hóng xuē
青巾玉带红靴
xī shān hǎo chù biàn wéi jiā
溪山好处便为家
shéi zhī bā xiá lù
谁知巴峡路
què jiàn luò chéng huā
却见洛城花

miàn xuán luò yīng fēi yù ruǐ
面旋落英飞玉蕊
rén jiān chūn rì chū xié
人间春日初斜
shí nián bù jiàn zǐ yún chē
十年不见紫云车
lóng qiū xīn dòng fǔ
龙丘新洞府
qiān dǐng yǎng dān shā
铅鼎养丹砂

II

*Lord Long Qiu traveled to Bashu from Luoyang, accompanied
by two maidservants in martial attire, riding handsome horses.
Where streams and mountains were scenic, they lingered a while.
Those who saw them thought they were from another world. Ten
years later, Lord Long Qiu had a house built north of Huanggang,
called himself the Serene Gentleman. This poem records this
episode.*

Two handmaidens rode off on fine horses
blue scarves jade belts scarlet boots
camped beside scenic streams in the mountains
Who knew on the gorge road to Baxia
would appear flowers from Luoyang

Whirling petals and jade stamens in the wind
their faces were lit by the first light of spring
vanished for ten years following a purple-cloud chariot
In Long Qiu's latest secret chamber
they stir cinnabar in a lead cauldron

三

yè yǐn dōng pō xǐng fù zuì
夜饮东坡醒复醉
guī lái fǎng fú sān gēng
归来仿佛三更
jiā tóng bí xī yǐ léi míng
家童鼻息已雷鸣
qiāo mén dū bù yìng
敲门都不应
yǐ zhàng tīng jiāng shēng
倚杖听江声

cháng hèn cǐ shēn fēi wǒ yǒu
长恨此身非我有
hé shí wàng què yíng yíng
何时忘却营营
yè lán fēng jìng hú wén píng
夜阑风静縠纹平
xiǎo zhōu cóng cǐ shì
小舟从此逝
jiāng hǎi jì yú shēng
江海寄余生

III

Sobered and got drunk again at East Hill
I stumbled home in the dead of night
The houseboy's snore thunders
No one answers my knocking on the door
I lean on my cane and listen to the river

I have long hated not owning my body
When does one forget worldly labor
Night deepens as wind calms water's rippling silk
My small boat shall vanish from here
to travel life in rivers and seas

mǎn jiāng hóng
满江红

jì è zhōu zhū shǐ jūn shòu chāng
寄鄂州朱使君寿昌

jiāng hàn xī lái
江汉西来
gāo lóu xià
高楼下
pú táo shēn bì
蒲萄深碧
yóu zì dài
犹自带
mín é xuě làng
岷峨雪浪
jǐn jiāng chūn sè
锦江春色
jūn shì nán shān yí ài shǒu
君是南山遗爱守
wǒ wéi jiàn wài sī guī kè
我为剑外思归客
duì cǐ jiān
对此间
fēng wù qǐ wú qíng
风物岂无情
yīn qín shuō
殷勤说

To the Tune of
"The River Turns Red"

To Governor Zhu Shou-Chang of Ezhou

Rivers Yangtze and Han dash from the west
Waves beneath the tower
churn the dark green of grapes
stir memories of snow
on Min and Emei Mountains
splash spring colors from Satin River
You the beloved ex-judge of South Mountains
and I a homesick guest beyond the Sword Gate
linger here
moved by the windswept scene
Words rush my lips

jiāng biǎo zhuàn
江表传

jūn xiū dú
君休读

kuáng chǔ shì
狂处士

zhēn kān xī
真堪惜

kōng zhōu duì yīng wǔ
空州对鹦鹉

wěi huā xiāo sè
苇花萧瑟

bù dú xiào shū shēng zhēng dǐ shì
不独笑书生争底事

cáo gōng huáng zǔ jù piāo hū
曹公黄祖俱飘忽

yuàn shǐ jūn
愿使君

hái fù zhé xiān shī
还赋谪仙诗

zhuī huáng hè
追黄鹤

No need to read a biography
of Three Kingdom's mad heroes
Such a wild sage
What a waste
A parrot landed on an empty island
Reed blossoms wither and sing
What a laugh for a scholar to fight
warlords who would vanish like smoke
You should write a poem
befitting the exiled god
Match *The Golden Crane*

nán gē zi
南歌子

一

shān yǔ gē méi liǎn
山与歌眉敛
bō tóng zuì yǎn liú
波同醉眼流
yóu rén dōu shàng shí sān lóu
游人都上十三楼
bù xiàn zhú xī gē chuī
不羡竹西歌吹
gǔ yáng zhōu
古扬州

gū shǔ lián chāng chù
菰黍联昌歜
qióng yí dào yù zhōu
琼彝倒玉舟
shéi jiā shuǐ diào chàng gē tóu
谁家水调唱歌头
shēng rào bì shān fēi qù
声绕碧山飞去
wǎn yún liú
晚云留

To the Tune of "Southern Song"

I

Courtesans' eyebrows mirror shades of distant
    mountains
Waves shimmer in the lake and their drunken eyes
Every visitor ascends the terrace of Thirteen Room
    Mansion
Forget Bamboo-West Pavilion haunted by flutes
in ancient Yangzhou

Wild grain cakes are stuffed with marinated calamus
    roots
Wine flows from jade jars into jeweled chalices
The sound of someone singing the Water Tune
wraps around emerald mountains and flies away
Evening clouds remain

二

dài jiǔ chōng shān yǔ
带酒冲山雨
hé yī shuì wǎn qíng
和衣睡晚晴
bù zhī zhōng gǔ bào tiān míng
不知钟鼓报天明
mèng lǐ xǔ rán hú dié
梦里栩然蝴蝶
yī shēn qīng
一身轻

lǎo qù cái dōu jìn
老去才都尽
guī lái jì wèi chéng
归来计未成
qiú tián wèn shě xiào háo yīng
求田问舍笑豪英
zì' ài hú biān shā lù
自爱湖边沙路
miǎn ní xíng
免泥行

II

Carrying wine dashed through mountain rain
Slept with my clothes on till it cleared
Didn't hear bells and drums announce daybreak
In my dream I flew with butterfly wings
My body became weightless

My talents fade with the burden of age
My plan to go home remains foiled
I am looking for a farm the mighty can laugh
Haunt the lakeside sand path
No mud soils my walk

niàn nú jiāo
念奴娇

chì bì huái gǔ
赤壁怀古

dà jiāng dōng qù
大江东去
làng táo jìn
浪淘尽
qiān gǔ fēng liú rén wù
千古风流人物
gù lěi xī biān
故垒西边
rén dào shì
人道是
sān guó zhōu láng chì bì
三国周郎赤壁
luàn shí bēng yún
乱石崩云
jīng tāo liè àn
惊涛裂岸
juǎn qǐ qiān duī xuě
卷起千堆雪
jiāng shān rú huà
江山如画
yī shí duō shǎo háo jié
一时多少豪杰

To the Tune of "Nian Nu's Charm"

Remembrance at Red Cliffs

The vast river rushes eastward
Waves have washed away all the dashing
men for a thousand years
To the west of the old fortress
they say are the Red Cliffs
of Three-Kingdoms' Lord Zhou
Chaos of rocks split the clouds
Sudden billows lash the shore
pile up a thousand heaps of snow
The vivid scene of mountain-flanked river
once home to countless heroes

yáo xiǎng gōng jǐn dāng nián
遥想公瑾当年
xiǎo qiáo chū jià liǎo
小乔初嫁了
xióng zī yīng fā
雄姿英发
yǔ shàn guān jīn
羽扇纶巾
tán xiào jiān
谈笑间
qiáng lǔ huī fēi yān miè
樯橹灰飞烟灭
gù guó shén yóu
故国神游
duō qíng yīng xiào wǒ
多情应笑我
zǎo shēng huá fà
早生华发
rén jiān rú mèng
人间如梦
yī zūn hái lèi jiāng yuè
一樽还酹江月

I can see Lord Zhou in his youth
with lovely Xiao Qiao newly wed
A strapping warrior in a silk-ribbon hat
shaking a white feather fan
chatting and laughing
as enemy ships burned to ashes
My spirit traveling in ancient kingdoms
I am laughable burdened with sentiments
White hairs bloom before they are due
Life is a dream
I offer a cup of wine to the river moon

qìn yuán chūn

沁园春

fù mì zhōu zǎo xíng mǎ shàng jì zi yóu
赴密州早行马上寄子由

gū guǎn dēng qīng
孤馆灯青

yě diàn jī hào
野店鸡号

lǚ zhěn mèng cán
旅枕梦残

jiàn yuè huá shōu liàn
渐月华收练

chén shuāng gěng gěng
晨霜耿耿

yún shān chī jǐn
云山摛锦

zhāo lù tuán tuán
朝露溥溥

shì lù wú qióng
世路无穷

láo shēng yǒu xiàn
劳生有限

shì cǐ qūqū cháng xiān huān
似此区区长鲜欢

wēi yín bà
微吟罢

píng zhēng ān wú yǔ
凭征鞍无语

wǎng shì qiān duān
往事千端

To the Tune of "Spring in Qin Garden"

En route to Mizhou at dawn on horseback, for my brother Zi-You.

An oil lamp's blue flame haunts a lone lodge
Roosters crow into the open field
Dream shatters on the traveler's pillow
In stealth the moon withdraws lustrous ribbons
Dawn frost glitters as brocade spreads
over cloud-draped mountains
Morning dew lights up
The world's path never ends
A life of toil is bound by limits
Much ado with long absence of joy
I chant a little poetry then stop
lean on the saddle speechless
The past flashes in a thousand scenes

dāng shí gòng kè cháng'ān
当时共客长安
shì èr lù chū lái jù shào nián
似二陆初来俱少年
yǒu bǐ tóu qiān zì
有笔头千字
xiōng zhōng wàn juǎn
胸中万卷
zhì jūn yáo shùn
致君尧舜
cǐ shì hé nán
此事何难
yòng shě yóu shí
用舍由时
xíng cáng zài wǒ
行藏在我
xiù shǒu hé fáng xián chù kàn
袖手何妨闲处看
shēn cháng jiàn
身长健
dàn yōu yóu zú suì
但优游卒岁
qiě dòu zūn qián
且斗尊前

We once lodged together in Chang-an
Just like when Lu Brothers were young
Thousands of words flew from our brushes
Ten thousand scrolls in our chests
to guide the emperor to ancient ideals
How hard could that be
Employed or not depends on the times
Action or seclusion is up to us
Let's fold our arms and observe the quiet
Live long and thrive
Roam at leisure year after year
Delight in the sight of goblets

鹊桥仙

七夕送陈令举

缑山仙子
高情云渺
不学痴牛騃女
凤箫声断月明中
举手谢时人欲去

客槎曾犯
银河波浪
尚带天风海雨
相逢一醉是前缘
风雨散
飘然何处

To the Tune of
"Celestials on the Bridge of Magpies"

Farewell to Chen Ling-Ju on the Night of Sevens

The prince on Gou Mountain
adopted the clouds' point of view
unlike the lovesick Cowherd and Weaving Girl
He stopped playing the phoenix flute in moonglow
raised his hands in farewell and ascended

Waves churned in the Milky Way
as we sailed past the Cowherd
The boat retains the celestial wind and ocean rain
Destiny brought us to meet over wine
The wind and rain disperse
Where shall each of us drift

如梦令

为向东坡传语

人在玉堂深处

别后有谁来

雪压小桥无路

归去

归去

江上一犁春雨

To the Tune of "A Dream Song"

Pass the word to East Hill
I wander jade halls of Imperial Academy
Who has visited since I left
Has snow buried the little bridge
I shall return
Return
in plough-deep spring rain by the river

水龙吟

次韵章质夫杨花词

似花还似非花

也无人惜从教坠

抛家傍路

思量却是

无情有思

萦损柔肠

困酣娇眼

欲开还闭

梦随风万里

寻郎去处

又还被

莺呼起

To the Tune of "Water Dragon Chant"

Adopting the Rhymes of Zhang Zhi-Fu's Tune Poem on Poplar Flowers

They are flowers yet unlike any
No one pities the catkins falling
abandoning home for the roadside
I contemplate this
Thoughts without feeling
My tender insides twist
Sleep locks my irresistible eyes
They refuse to open
My dream rides the wind ten thousand miles
to track down my man
until suddenly
an oriole calls

bù hèn cǐ huā fēi jìn
不恨此花飞尽

hèn xī yuán
恨西园

luò hóng nán zhuì
落红难缀

xiǎo lái yǔ guò
晓来雨过

yí zōng hé zài
遗踪何在

yī chí píng suì
一池萍碎

chūn sè sān fēn
春色三分

èr fēn chén tǔ
二分尘土

yī fēn liú shuǐ
一分流水

xì kàn lái
细看来

bù shì yáng huā
不是杨花

diǎn diǎn shì lí rén lèi
点点是离人泪

I don't regret the catkins' vanishing flight
only the west garden where
fallen red blossoms can't be stitched back
After morning rain
I look for them
in a pond covered by duckweed
Spring split into three parts
Two parts dust
One part lapping water
I lean close to look
No poplar flowers
Only countless tears of separation

wàng jiāng nán
望江南

chāo rán tái zuò
超然台作

chūn wèi lǎo
春未老
fēng xì liǔ xié xié
风细柳斜斜
shì shàng chāo rán tái shàng kàn
试上超然台上看
bàn háo chūn shuǐ yī chéng huā
半壕春水一城花
yān yǔ àn qiān jiā
烟雨暗千家

hán shí hòu
寒食后
jiǔ xǐng què zī jiē
酒醒却咨嗟
xiū duì gù rén sī gù guó
休对故人思故国
qiě jiāng xīn huǒ shì xīn chá
且将新火试新茶
shī jiǔ chèn nián huá
诗酒趁年华

To the Tune of
"Gazing Southward of the Yangtze"

Written on Transcendence Terrace

Spring is not yet over
A thin wind combs willow strands
I climb Transcendence Terrace to see
half a moat of crystal water and a blossom-filled city
Foggy rain darkens a thousand houses

After Cold Food Day
I woke from wine and sighed
Do not pine with old friends for the ancestral home
Kindle new fire to try the new tea
Poetry and wine while the year blooms

xī jiāng yuè
西江月

一

píng shān táng
平山堂

sān guò píng shān táng xià
三过平山堂下
bàn shēng tán zhǐ shēng zhōng
半生弹指声中
shí nián bù jiàn lǎo xiān wēng
十年不见老仙翁
bì shàng lóng shé fēi dòng
壁上龙蛇飞动

yù diào wén zhāng tài shǒu
欲吊文章太守
réng gē yáng liǔ chūn fēng
仍歌杨柳春风
xiū yán wàn shì zhuǎn tóu kōng
休言万事转头空
wèi zhuǎn tóu shí jiē mèng
未转头时皆梦

To the Tune of "West River Moon"

I

Pingshan Hall

I pass by Pingshan Hall for the third time
Half a lifetime has elapsed in a finger snap
The celestial old man left ten years ago
Dragons dance in his handwriting on the wall

I mourn the learned governor as courtesans sing
his poem of wispy willows in spring wind
Don't say ten thousand things vanish as my head turns
It is already a dream before my head turns

二

sòng qián dài zhì
送钱待制

mò tàn píng yuán luò luò
莫叹平原落落
qiě yīng qù lǔ chí chí
且应去鲁迟迟
yǔ jūn gè jì shào nián shí
与君各记少年时
xū xìn rén shēng rú jì
须信人生如寄

bái fà qiān jīng xiāng sòng
白发千茎相送
shēn bēi bǎi fá xiū cí
深杯百罚休辞
pāi fú hé yòng jiǔ wéi chí
拍浮何用酒为池
wǒ yǐ wèi jūn dé zuì
我已为君德醉

II

For Qian Dai-Zhi

Do not sigh over the desolate prairie
Linger before you leave for Lu
We remember the fire of youth
understand life as a brief lodging

My thousand stems of white hair salute you
I fine you a hundred deep cups of wine
Who needs to float in a pond of wine
I am utterly drunk on account of you

三

重九

diǎn diǎn lóu tóu xì yǔ
点点楼头细雨
chóng chóng jiāng wài píng hú
重重江外平湖
dāng nián xì mǎ huì dōng xú
当年戏马会东徐
jīn zhāo qī liáng nán pǔ
今朝凄凉南浦

mò hèn huáng huā wèi tǔ
莫恨黄花未吐
qiě jiào hóng fěn xiāng fú
且教红粉相扶
jiǔ lán bù bì kàn zhū yú
酒阑不必看茱萸
fǔ yǎng rén jiān jīn gǔ
俯仰人间今古

III

Double Ninth

A small rain patters on the balcony
A smooth lake hides beyond the shrouded river
Once we met on Equestrian Terrace in East Xu
Now I sink alone into the cold on South Shore

Don't regret chrysanthemums' failure to bloom
A rouged beauty steps forward to take my arm
No need to seek the lucky dogwood after wine
Mortals have endured ups and downs since time began

四

顷在黄州，春夜行蕲水中，过酒家饮，酒醉，乘月至一溪桥上，解鞍，曲肱醉卧少休。及觉已晓，乱山攒拥，流水锵然，疑非尘世也。书此语桥柱上。

zhào yě mí mí qiǎn làng
照野弥弥浅浪
héng kōng yǐn yǐn céng xiāo
横空隐隐层霄
zhàng ní wèi jiě yù cōng jiāo
障泥未解玉骢骄
wǒ yù zuì mián fāng cǎo
我欲醉眠芳草

kě xī yī xī fēng yuè
可惜一溪风月
mò jiào tà pò qióng yáo
莫教踏破琼瑶
jiě ān yī zhěn lù yáng qiáo
解鞍欹枕绿杨桥
dù yǔ yī shēng chūn xiǎo
杜宇一声春晓

IV

Soon after I arrived in Huangzhou, I wandered along the Qi River on a spring night. Passed a wine-house, got drunk, went to a bridge over a stream by moonlight. Untied the saddle, curled up in drunken sleep for a little rest. When I woke up, it was dawn. Mountains surged all around me, rushing water chimed. I wondered if I were no longer in the world of mortals. I wrote this poem on a column on the bridge.

An open field shimmered with shallow waves
The sky hinted at vast terraces of clouds
Suddenly my white horse jerked me on the saddle
I wanted to sleep off the wine in fragrant grass

The wind and moon beckoned from the stream
I didn't dare break the dazzling jade
untied the saddle for a pillow on green poplar bridge
A cuckoo sounded the spring daybreak

xíng xiāng zǐ

行香子

一

qīng yè wú chén

清夜无尘

yuè sè rú yín

月色如银

jiǔ zhēn shí

酒斟时

xū mǎn shí fēn

须满十分

fú míng fú lì

浮名浮利

xū kǔ láo shén

虚苦劳神

tàn xì zhōng jū

叹隙中驹

shí zhōng huǒ

石中火

mèng zhōng shēn

梦中身

To the Tune of "Journey Through Incense"

I

A crystal night untouched by dust
fills with silver moonlight
Let wine overflow goblets
Fame and wealth drift
waste the spirit in blind labor
Life passes as a sunbeam
galloping over a crack in the wall
Flames leaping from a firestone
My body is locked in a dream

suī bào wén zhāng
虽抱文章

kāi kǒu shéi qīn
开口谁亲

qiě táo táo
且陶陶

lè jìn tiān zhēn
乐尽天真

jǐ shí guī qù
几时归去

zuò gè xián rén
作个闲人

duì yī zhāng qín
对一张琴

yī hú jiǔ
一壶酒

yī xī yún
一溪云

My chest swells with erudition
My mouth opens with no one to impress
Let me delight
in true simplicity
Someday I shall return home
to indulge in leisure
pluck strings of guqin
beside a flask of wine
a stream haunted by clouds

二

xié shǒu jiāng cūn
携手江村
méi xuě piāo qún
梅雪飘裙
qíng hé xiàn
情何限
chù chù xiāo hún
处处消魂
gù rén bù jiàn
故人不见
jiù qǔ chóng wén
旧曲重闻
xiàng wàng hú lóu
向望湖楼
gū shān sì
孤山寺
yǒng jīn mén
涌金门

II

To Shu Gu from Danyang City

Arm in arm we roamed the riverside village
Plum petals covered our clothes with snow
Our elation knew no limits
Everywhere we were spellbound
Now in my absence you hear
the same old tunes
Gazing at Lakeview Tower
Lone Mountain Temple
Rushing Gold Gate

xún cháng xíng chù
寻常行处

tí shī qiān shǒu
题诗千首

xiù luó shān
绣罗衫

yǔ fú hóng chén
与拂红尘

bié lái xiāng yì
别来相忆

zhī shì hé rén
知是何人

yǒu hú zhōng yuè
有湖中月

jiāng biān liǔ
江边柳

lǒng tóu yún
陇头云

We haunted those places
inscribed a thousand poems
Now someone dusts them off
with her red sleeve of embroidered silk
Have I been missed since I left
I know who recalls it all
The moon in West Lake
Willows along the river
Clouds atop mountains

三

guò qī lǐ lài
过七里濑

yī yè zhōu qīng
一叶舟轻
shuāng jiǎng hóng jīng
双桨鸿惊
shuǐ tiān qīng
水天清
yǐng zhàn bō píng
影湛波平
yú fān zǎo jiàn
鱼翻藻鉴
lù diǎn yān tīng
鹭点烟汀
guò shā xī jí
过沙溪急
shuāng xī lěng
霜溪冷
yuè xī míng
月溪明

III

Passing Through the Seven-li Rapid

I ride a leaf of a boat
My oars startle the geese
The water clear as the sky
Sharp reflections ink smooth waves
A fish breaks the algae-embroidered mirror
A heron marks the misted bank
The river rushes past the sand
chills the frosted shores
glistens beneath the moon

chóng chóng shì huà

重重似画

qū qū rú píng

曲曲如屏

suàn dāng nián

算当年

xū lǎo yán líng

虚老严陵

jūn chén yī mèng

君臣一梦

jīn gǔ kōng míng

今古空名

dàn yuǎn shān cháng

但远山长

yún shān luàn

云山乱

xiǎo shān qīng

晓山青

Ridge upon ridge animate a painting
Bend after bend make a folded screen
I picture Yan Guang a thousand years ago
growing old in vain
The emperor sought him out
An empty dream for the history books
Only mountains stretch on forever
blend with sunset clouds
wake to green each dawn

阳关曲
yáng guān qǔ

中秋月
zhōng qiū yuè

暮云收尽溢清寒
mù yún shōu jìn yì qīng hán

银汉无声转玉盘
yín hàn wú shēng zhuàn yù pán

此生此夜不长好
cǐ shēng cǐ yè bù cháng hǎo

明月明年何处看
míng yuè míng nián hé chù kàn

To the Tune of
"The Sun Pass"

Mid Autumn Moon

Dusk clouds vanish as a crystal chill blooms
The moon's jade plate turns against the soundless Milky
    Way
This life this night is a flower about to fade
Where will we see this lustrous moon next year

永遇乐

彭城夜宿燕子楼，梦盼盼，因作此词。

míng yuè rú shuāng
明月如霜

hǎo fēng rú shuǐ
好风如水

qīng jǐng wú xiàn
清景无限

qū gǎng tiào yú
曲港跳鱼

yuán hé xiè lù
圆荷泻露

jì mò wú rén jiàn
寂寞无人见

dǎn rú sān gǔ
紞如三鼓

kēng rán yī yè
铿然一叶

àn àn mèng yún jīng duàn
黯黯梦云惊断

yè máng máng
夜茫茫

chóng xún wú chù
重寻无处

jué lái xiǎo yuán xíng biàn
觉来小园行遍

To the Tune of "Eternal Happiness"

I spent the night in Swallow Mansion in Peng City. Dreamed of Pan-Pan, and wrote this poem.

Moonlight frosts the night
A crisp wind summons water
Lucid landscape without end
Fish leap in the sinuous harbor
Dew spills from lotus leaves
Deep silence beyond human ears
The third watch drum resounds
Clang   a leaf falls
Darkly my dream clouds break
Night has no bounds
I try in vain to renew the dream
wake to pace a little garden

tiān yá juàn kè
天涯倦客
shān zhōng guī lù
山中归路
wàng duàn gù yuán xīn yǎn
望断故园心眼
yàn zi lóu kōng
燕子楼空
jiā rén hé zài
佳人何在
kōng suǒ lóu zhōng yàn
空锁楼中燕
gǔ jīn rú mèng
古今如梦
hé céng mèng jué
何曾梦觉
dàn yǒu jiù huān xīn yuàn
但有旧欢新怨
yì shí duì
异时对
huáng lóu yè jǐng
黄楼夜景
wèi yú hào tàn
为余浩叹

A tired traveler at the sky's edge
Mountains conceal my way home
My mind's eye fixates on journey's end
Swallow Mansion emptied
The lithe beauty is no more
Why lock swallows in the mansion
An ancient dream lives on
We never wake from the dream
of old bliss and new misery
Someday someone will dwell
in the night magic of Yellow Mansion
heave a sigh over my passing

zhāo jūn yuàn

昭君怨

jīn shān sòng liǔ zi yù

金山送柳子玉

shéi zuò huán yī sān nòng

谁作桓伊三弄

jīng pò lù chuāng yōu mèng

惊破绿窗幽梦

xīn yuè yǔ chóu yān

新月与愁烟

mǎn jiāng tiān

满江天

yù qù yòu hái bù qù

欲去又还不去

míng rì luò huā fēi xù

明日落花飞絮

fēi xù sòng xíng zhōu

飞絮送行舟

shuǐ dōng liú

水东流

To the Tune of "Zhao Jun's Regret"

Seeing off Liu Zi-Yu at Gold Mountain

Someone channeled Huan Yi in three flute rounds
shattered a deep dream behind the green window gauze
The crescent is misted by sadness
The sky fills the river

You almost leave yet cannot
Tomorrow blossoms will rain into flying catkin fuzz
Catkin fuzz will follow your boat in farewell
The river rushes east as always

zhè gū tiān
鹧鸪天

lín duàn shān míng zhú yǐn qiáng
林断山明竹隐墙
luàn chán shuāi cǎo xiǎo chí táng
乱蝉衰草小池塘
fān kōng bái niǎo shí shí jiàn
翻空白鸟时时见
zhào shuǐ hóng qú xì xì xiāng
照水红蕖细细香

cūn shě wài
村舍外
gǔ chéng páng
古城旁
zhàng lí xú bù zhuǎn xié yáng
杖藜徐步转斜阳
yīn qín zuó yè sān gēng yǔ
殷勤昨夜三更雨
yòu dé fú shēng yī rì liáng
又得浮生一日凉

To the Tune of "Partridge Sky"

The forest ends the mountain gleams bamboos hide
    walls
Cicadas cry withered grass around a little pond
Now and then a white bird soars into the sky
Red lotuses brighten the water in a subtle perfume

Beyond village huts
Beside an ancient town
I pace with a walking stick as the sun begins to set
How considerate of the third watch rain last night
Another cool day in this floating life

yú fù
渔父　　　　　（四首）

yú fù yǐn
渔父饮
shéi jiā qù
谁家去
yú xiè yī shí fēn fù
鱼蟹一时分付
jiǔ wú duō shǎo zuì wéi qī
酒无多少醉为期
bǐ cǐ bù lùn qián shù
彼此不论钱数

又

yú fù zuì
渔父醉
suō yī wǔ
蓑衣舞
zuì lǐ què xún guī lù
醉里却寻归路
qīng zhōu duǎn zhào rèn xié héng
轻舟短棹任斜横
xǐng hòu bù zhī hé chù
醒后不知何处

To the Tune of
"The Fisherman"

I

The fisherman needs a drink
Which wine house will he visit?
With fish and crabs he pays for wine
not measured   intoxication sets the limit
Money doesn't enter the bargain

II

The drunken fisherman dances
in a raincape of palm bark
He seeks the return path
jabs with the oars in his flimsy boat
When sobers up doesn't know where he is

又

渔父醒

春江午

梦断落花飞絮

酒醒还醉醉还醒

一笑人间今古

又

渔父笑

轻鸥举

漠漠一江风雨

江边骑马是官人

借我孤舟南渡

III

The fisherman wakes at noon
on the river in spring
His dream broke in falling blossoms and catkin fuzz
Sober then drunk   drunk then sober
he laughs at the history of mortals

IV

The fisherman laughs
Gulls rise without effort
The river merges with endless wind and rain
An official on horseback at the river's edge
asks to be ferried south on the lone boat

Notes

p. 2: This is one of the best-known poems by Su Dong-Po. He may have composed this poem after being demoted to Huizhou in 1094. It has been recorded that he asked his beloved companion Chao-Yun to sing this tune poem to him after he composed it. She burst into tears while singing the lines about the willow catkins and the sweet-scented grass at the sky's edge. The sky's edge (天涯) refers to a remote place, such as Huizhou. A sweet-scented grass (芳草) refers to a person of integrity.

p. 4: Gaotang refers to Gaotang Temple, or Gaotang Terrace, where two kings of the Kingdom of Chu, from different times, dreamed of intimate meetings with the Goddess of Wu Mountain (巫山神女). She has since become the symbol for the ultimate object of desire. According to *The New History of the Tang Dynasty* (新唐书), the second daughter of Dou Yi and Princess Xiang Yang was famed for her beauty, courage, and wisdom. Her parents held an archery competition to choose a husband for her from her numerous suitors. The targets were the eyes of a peacock painted on a screen. Li Yuan (566-635 A.D.) won the competition. He later became the Tang Dynasty Founding Emperor, Tang Gao Zu (唐高祖). Subsequently, "painted screen (画屏)" alludes to the choosing of a husband.

p. 6: Su Dong-Po may have composed this poem around 1078. Li Gong-Ze, or Li Chang, was an old friend of Su Dong-Po's. They both served in the government, held similar political views, for which they were both demoted at various times. They met up numerous times, whenever they could. Each time they drank wine, composed poems, and talked deep into the night. The line about the lost soul alludes to the poem "Summoning the Soul (招魂)" by Qu Yuan (352-281 B.C.). Here Dong-Po referred to the fact that both he and Gong-Ze were waiting for the emperor to summon them to serve the country in a greater capacity.

p. 8: Su Dong-Po composed this poem in 1074, at Jingkou, the site of an ancient capital. North Mountain is to the northeast of Jingkou, facing the Yangtze River.

p. 10: Su Dong-Po was transferred from being the judge in the prosperous Hangzhou to being the governor of the destitute Mizhou in the autumn of 1074. He wrote this poem the following year on the fifteenth of the first month (lunar calendar), on the day of the Lantern Festival. Snow was believed to foretell a good harvest later in the year, which Dong-Po hoped for.

p. 12: Zhang Wo-Quan was demoted to Huangzhou, but adapted in serenity. He built a pavilion by the Yangtze River, near his house. Su Dong-Po was also demoted to Huangzhou, and achieved the same mind set. He admired the beauty of the Yantze River, and Zhang Wo-Quan's temperament, so he named this pavilion and gifted Wo-Quan with this poem in 1083. The "Old Drunkard" refers to Dong-Po's mentor Eu-Yang Xiu. One qing (顷) is approximately 16.5 acres. Lord Lan Tai refers to Song Yu (~298 - ~222 B.C.), Qu Yuan's student, famous for his poetry. The philosopher and writer

Zhuang Zi (~369 - ~286 B.C.) was the representative of Taoism second only to its founder Lao Zi (604-531 B.C.).

p. 16: This is one of the best-known poems by Su Dong-Po. He composed it on the Mid Autumn Festival in 1076, when he was the governor of Mizhou. Bing Chen was the fifty-third year in the sixty-year cycle used in ancient Chinese calendar.

p. 20: Tui-Zhi refers to the Tang Dynasty poet Han Yu (768-824 A.D.). Master Ying was a monk renowned for his skills in playing guqin, a seven-stringed instrument with over three thousand years of history in China.

p. 24: Xu Jun-You was the governor of Huangzhou when Su Dong-Po was demoted there in 1080. In a letter to his brother Zi-You, Dong-Po reported that Jun-You welcomed him with open arms, and treated him as family. Dong-Po wrote this poem during a banquet on Hanhui Terrace hosted by Jun-You, on the Festival of Double Ninth, held on the ninth day of the ninth lunar month.

p. 26: Su Dong-Po composed this poem during one of the banquets held in his honor by Xu Jun-You (the governor of Huangzhou). He took all the lines in this poem from poems by Tang Dynasty poets, except for the two-word lines (fourth and ninth lines), as follows:
Line 1: "Regret Over Spring (惜春)", by Du Mu.
Line 2: "Nine Casual Poems (绝句漫兴九首)", by Du Fu.
Line 3: "Seeing-off a Friend at the Bamboo Forest Temple (竹林寺别友人)" by Xu Hun.
Line 5: "Seeing-off Han Qi-Zhong at Luozhong, on His

Way to Become the Governor's Deputy in Wuxing (洛中送韩七中丞之吴兴)" by Liu Yu-Xi.

Line 6: "Returning Late from Jinchang on Horseback (晋昌晚归马上赠)" by Li Shang-Yin.

Line 7: "Pondering the Journey Home Upon the Ancient Royal Terrace of Yue on a Winter Day (冬日登越王台怀归)" by Xu Hun.

Line 8: "Long Lines with Four Rhymes on the Twelfth Day of the Eighth Month, on the Occasion of Having Been Relieved of Duty and Moved to Zha River House (八月十二日得替后移居霅溪馆因题长句四韵)" by Du Mu.

Line 10: "Untitled (无题)" beginning with the line "Soughing East Wind Brings Drizzling Rain (飒飒东风细雨来)" by Li Shang-Yin.

p. 28: Chen Shu-Gu was a close friend of Su Dong-Po's. They worked together in Hangzhou from 1072 to 1074. When Shu-Gu was transferred from Hangzhou in 1074, Dong-Po saw him off all the way to Linping, northeast of Hangzhou, and composed this poem for him.

p. 30: Su Dong-Po composed this poem at Lingao Pavilion in Huangzhou in 1081. Min Mountain and Emei Mountain are located in Dong-Po's hometown Meishan.

p. 32: Su Dong-Po wrote this in 1082, his third year of demotion in Huangzhou. Thirty li southeast of Huangzhou, there was a little town called Sandy Lake, where Dong-Po intended to buy some land. He traveled there to look over the land, and it rained on the way, which inspired this poem.

p. 34: Wang Ding-Guo was Su Dong-Po's student. When Dong-Po was imprisoned in 1079 because of the Crow Terrace Poetry Case, Ding-Guo was punished for collecting Dong-Po's poems. Ding-Guo was demoted and transferred to the remote and impoverished Binzhou south of Dayu Mountain (岭南) for three years, accompanied by the courtesan Rou-Nu. Dong-Po composed this poem in appreciation of Rou-Nu.

p. 36: Su Dong-Po composed this in 1083, during his demotion in Huangzhou.

p. 40: Su Dong-Po likely composed this in 1082, during his demotion in Huangzhou. The three lines "For one hundred years/ let me get drunk/ thirty six thousand times" originated from Li Bai's poem, Song of Xiangyang (襄阳歌): "One hundred years — thirty six thousand days, each day you must pour three hundred cups (百年三万六千日，一日须倾三百杯)".

p. 44: Su Dong-Po wrote this in 1084, four years after being demoted to Huangzhou, when he was transferred to Ruzhou, which is much closer to the capital, and near the Luo River. The first line of this poem was taken from the opening line of the poem by Tao Yuan-Ming (~365-427 A.D.), "Returning to Where One Belongs (归去来兮辞)".

p. 48: There was a devastating spring draught in Xuzhou in 1078. As the governor of Xuzhou, Su Dong-Po traveled to Stone Pond to pray for rain, and then again to give thanks after it rained. He composed five poems to the tune of Sand of Washing Stream during the trip to give thanks after rain at Stone Pond. This was the first poem in the sequence.

p. 50: Su Dong-Po wrote this poem in 1082, during his demotion in Huangzhou. The last line alludes to a poem by Tang Dynasty poet Bai Ju-Yi (772-846 A.D.), "The Drunken Song (醉歌)", in which the golden rooster hastening daybreak was used to symbolize the brevity of life.

p. 52: This was the second poem in the five-poem sequence to the tune of Sand of the Washing Stream that So Dong-Po wrote in 1078, while he was the governor of Xuzhou, during the trip to Stone Pond to give thanks for rain.

p. 54: Su Dong-Po composed this poem in the winter of 1082, during his demotion in Huangzhou.

p. 56: This was the last in the five-poem sequence to the tune of Sand of the Washing Stream that Su Dong-Po wrote in 1078, during the trip to Stone Pond to give thanks for rain, as the governor of Xuzhou. "Plowing side by side" alludes to the story of two hermits who retired from politics to plow side by side; Confucius and his disciples came upon them while traveling.

p. 58: This was the fourth poem in the five-poem sequence to the tune of Sand of the Washing Stream that Su Dong-Po wrote in 1078, during the trip to Stone Pond to give thanks for rain, as the governor of Xuzhou.

p. 60: Su Dong-Po probably composed this poem in the spring of 1066, the year after his first wife Wang Fu died. Lord Shen refers to the poet Shen Yue (441-513 A.D.), who described in a letter to a friend how he had to tighten his belt as he grew thin from illness.

p. 62: When Su Dong-Po was eighteen, he married beautiful Wang Fu, who was sixteen years old. They were deeply in love with each other, and Wang Fu was a perfect daughter-in-law to Dong-Po's parents. She died when she was only twenty-six. Dong-Po was devastated. On the tenth anniversary of her death in 1075, Dong-Po dreamed of her and composed this tune poem. He was the governor of Mizhou at the time. This is one of the most beloved poems by Su Dong-Po.

p. 66: Su Dong-Po composed this in 1074, when he was the judge in Hangzhou, and his close friend Chen Shu-Gu was about to be transferred away from his post as the governor of Hangzhou. "The Sun Pass" is the song with the famous poem by the Tang Dynasty poet Wang Wei, "Seeing Off Yuan Er to Anxi (送元二使安西)", as the lyric, which was customarily sung at farewell parties during the Song Dynasty.

p. 70: Su Dong-Po was transferred to Xuzhou to be its governor in 1077, then transferred again to Huzhou in 1979. He composed this poem in 1079, on his way from Xuzhou to Huzhou. Dong-Po loved Xuzhou, where he was a popular and beloved governor. This poem is still widely circulated among the people of Xuzhou. The Sui embankments refer to the riverbanks of the Bian River, an important waterway built during the Sui Dynasty (581-618 A.D.). The Third Month in the lunar calendar corresponds roughly to April.

p. 74: In 1080, when Su Dong-Po was forty-three years old, he was demoted to Huangzhou due to the Crow Terrace Poetry Case. In the first half of his second year there, he had trouble making ends meet. An old friend helped him request a few acres of land on East Hill beyond the east gate of Huangzhou, which was once a military campground. He farmed this land with his family to supplement daily needs, and named himself Dong-Po Ju Shi (Hermit of East Hill). It snowed that winter. Dong-Po built a hut at East Hill, and named it Snow Hall. When spring arrived outside Snow Hall on East Hill, Dong-Po was reminded of the poem by Tao Yuan-Ming, "Travel the Slant Valley (游斜川)". Zeng Cheng was the mountain north of Lu Mountains, named after the legendary peak of Kunlun Mountain, where the immortals were said to reside.

p. 78: Su Dong-Po wrote this poem around 1072-1074, when he was the judge in Hangzhou. Zhang Xian (990-1078 A.D.) was a famous poet of tune poems. The Xiang Princesses were E Huang and Nu Ying, daughters of Yao, the first great emperor in Chinese legend. Yao abdicated and made Shun the emperor, when he judged Shun to be a wise, hardworking, and loving leader of the people. Yao also married his two daughters to Shun. Shun later died during an inspection tour of the south. E Huang and Nu Ying traced his route for the tour, and were by the Xiang River when they heard the news of his death. Overcame by grief, they drowned themselves in the river, and became the Goddesses of the Xiang River. According to *Notes from the Ink Village* (墨庄漫录), by Zhang Bang-Ji toward the end of the Song Dynasty, when Dong-Po took some guests boating on the West Lake one day, they spotted an ornate boat on the lake, in which an exceedingly beautiful middle-aged woman was playing the string instrument zheng. Among Dong-Po's guests were two men in white robes for mourning, but they were so entranced by the woman's beauty that they could not take their eyes off her. Dong-Po composed this poem to tease them.

p. 82: Su Dong-Po wrote this tune poem in 1075, while he was the governor of Mizhou. He intended the style of this tune poem to counter that of the very popular tune poems by the poet Liu Yong, which were delicate, charming, and often decadent. "Lord Sun" refers to Sun Quan (182-252 A.D.), the founding emperor of East Wu, one of the three kingdoms of the Three Kingdoms period. He shot a tiger while on horseback, and killed the tiger even though it injured his horse. The Sky Wolf is the star Sirius, considered by the ancient Chinese to be the patron star of invaders.

p. 86: The Jade String refers to the two stars adjacent to the north of the star Yu Heng (the Jade Balance). Yu Heng is the star Alioth, the brightest star in the constellation Ursa Major, and the star on the handle of the Big Dipper closest to the dipper. West wind symbolizes the arrival of autumn.

p. 90: Su Dong-Po likely wrote this poem in 1091, when he was the governor of Hangzhou, and about to leave to become the Master of the Imperial Academy, the most prominent advisor to the emperor. Master Can Liao was the famous monk and poet Dao Qian, a close friend of Dong-Po's. Lord Xie refers to Xie An (320-385 A.D.), famous statesman and general from the East Jin period. Shortly before he died due to an illness, he passed through the West Gate of Yangzhou on the way back to the capital to see a doctor, and regretted that he would never be able to carry out his plan to return to seclusion in the East Mountain by following the Yangtze River in its seaward course. His nephew Yang Tan famously lamented his passing at the West Gate of Yangzhou. East Mountain has since become an allusion for seclusion. West Lake is in Hangzhou, located in the distant east from the capitol, not far from the coast.

p. 94: Su Dong-Po composed this poem in 1082, during his demotion in Huangzhou following his imprisonment due to the Crow Terrace Poetry Case, for which he was nearly executed.

p. 96: Su Dong-Po likely composed this poem in 1074.

p. 98: 薰风 (warm wind) refers to the southern wind that marks the beginning of summer. An ancient song called "Southern Wind (南风)" praises the warm southern wind for bringing the people happiness and prosperity. This was still performed during Su Dong-Po's time to celebrate the beginning of summer.

p. 100: Due to fundamental differences in political views with the prime minister, Su Dong-Po asked to be sent away to a post away from the capital in 1071. He was sent to Hangzhou as the judge. This was a happy time in his life, away from political strife and settled in beautiful Hangzhou, where everyone admired him as a poet. He was remarried after the death of his first wife, and was the father of young children. He wrote this poem in Runzhou, during his longest trip away from his family in Hangzhou. A pair of swallows symbolizes a happily married couple.

p. 102: In 1094, Su Dong-Po was demoted from Dingzhou near the northern border to Huizhou on the southern coast, over two thousand kilometers away, for the crime of "Mocking the Previous Reign". En route to Huizhou, he sailed east down the Yangtze to Jiujiang, near the scenic Lu Mountains. An old friend that he had not seen for many years, Su Jian (Bo-Gu), was sailing west up the Yangtze for his new post in Liyang. They met in Jiujiang, and parted in tears after a rushed reunion. Dong-Po gifted Bo-Gu with this tune poem. Thunder Lake was the ancient name for Lake Tai. "Gather up wet rice" (接淅) refers to Confucius' experience as told by his spiritual descendant Meng Zi. When Confucius and his disciples traveled to the Kingdom of Qi, they endured much hardship on the way. When they stopped to cook for themselves, they often had to depart suddenly to escape harassment before they were done washing the rice; they had to gather up the wet rice and run. Ling Jun refers to Qu Yuan (352-281 B.C.) from the Kingdom of Chu (which encompassed Liyang), the first great poet in the recorded history of China, who used the wild orchid to symbolize the sage. Meng-De was the Tang Dynasty poet Liu Yu-Xi (772-842 A.D.), another persecuted poet; he was demoted to the remote Wuling, and famous for composing the Bamboo Tunes (竹枝词), in emulation of the spirit of Qu Yuan's poetry. Liyang and Wuling were only a day's ride apart south of the Yangtze and west of Dongting Lake. Mo Yao is the Yao, an ethnic minority group in China, who resided in both Liyang and Wuling. One qing (顷) is approximately 16.5 acres.

p. 106: Su Dong-Po composed this poem while he was the governor of Hangzhou, probably inspired by a courtesan who arrived late at an official banquet and presented him with a sprig of pomegranate flowers. This poem follows in the tradition of Qu Yuan, who compared a sage awaiting his sovereign to summon him to serve the country to a neglected beauty and a fragrant orchid flower blooming in desolation.

p. 112: Su Dong-Po wrote this poem in 1091, while he was the governor of Hangzhou. Qian Mu-Fu was a descendent of the King of Wu Yue (928-971 A.D.), and a good friend of Dong-Po's. He was demoted thanks to political enemies in the imperial court. During the Tang and Song Dynasties, the hearth fire was renewed on Cold Food Day each year. "Knitting eyebrows" has the connotation of beautiful women, here courtesans. Xi Shi (506 B.C.-?) was one of the four most famous beauties in ancient China. She had a heart defect that often caused her to place her hands on her chest and knit her eyebrows. "Knitting eyebrows in imitation" has the opposite connotation.

p. 114: Lord Long Qiu refers to Su Dong-Po's good friend Chen Ji-Chang, who was known as a dashing wanderer in his youth, but lived a dull existence later in life. It was said that he built a house in Huanggang for esoteric pursuits, in order to hide from the loud shouting from his wife. Dong-Po wrote poems to tease him about it. This poem may be such an example.

p. 116: Su Dong-Po composed this in 1082, during his demotion in Huangzhou for the Crow Terrace Poetry Case. He lived in Lingao Pavilion by the Yangtze River, but farmed land at East Hill to help make ends meet. He also planted trees on East Hill, and built a hut there that he named Snow Hall, where he often drank with friends. This tune poem was so famous at the time that a rumor circulated about Dong-Po having hung up his official robes by the river, and departed in a boat with a long shout. Even the emperor heard about it and wondered.

p. 118: Su Dong-Po wrote this poem during his demotion in Huangzhou for his friend Zhu Shou-Chang, the governor of Ezhou, across the Yangtze from Huangzhou. The tower refers to Golden Crane Tower in Ezhou. Dong-Po's hometown Meishan is near the Sat-in River and the Min and Emei Mountains, and west of the Sword Gate. "South Mountains", located south of Chang-an, refers to Shanzhou, where Zhu was once the judge. "Wild sage" refers to Mi Heng (173-198 A.D.), famous for his poem "Ode to a Parrot". "Warlords" refer to Cao Cao (155-220 A.D.) and Huang Zhu. Cao Cao was a renowned warlord and poet. He tried to employ Mi Heng, who insulted him out of loyalty to the Han emperors' bloodline. Cao Cao passed Mi Heng along to Liu Biao (142-208 A.D.), a direct descendent of the Han emperors. Liu Biao's courtiers hated Mi Heng for his arrogance and rudeness. Liu Biao soon sent Mi Heng to one of his generals, Huang Zu, the governor of Jiangxia. At first, Huang Zhu treasured Mi Heng and admired his talent. Eventually, Mi Heng got drunk and insulted Huang Zhu, who immediately had him executed. Huang Zhu later regretted it and buried Mi Heng extravagantly on a sand isle, later known as Parrot Isle, visible from Golden Crane Tower. "The exiled god" refers to Li Bai, who greatly admired the poem "Upon the Golden Crane Tower" by a contemporary poet, Cui Hao.

p. 122: Su Dong-Po composed this tune poem in Hangzhou during his tenure there. He loved Hangzhou, and added to its beauty by constructing the famous dam (later known as Su Dam) that divided the West Lake in two, using the mud removed from the clogged lake. The Thirteen Room Mansion was a scenic landmark overlooking the West Lake, where Dong-Po often carried out his official duties as the judge, and later as the governor.

p. 124: Su Dong-Po composed this poem in the spring of 1082, during his demotion in Huangzhou due to the Crow Terrace Poetry Case. "Butterfly wings" refer to

Zhuang Zi's famous dream. When Zhuang Zi woke up from a dream in which he was a butterfly, he wondered if he was actually the butterfly dreaming of being a man.

p. 126: This is Su Dong-Po's best-known poem, referred to as "the timeless masterpiece (千古绝唱)" in classical Chinese literature. He composed it in 1082, during his demotion in Huangzhou. "Lord Zhou" refers to Zhou Yu (175-210 A.D.) from the end of the East Han period, nicknamed "Lord Zhou the Handsome". He was a sage, a scholar, and a famous general. He was best known for the Battle at Red Cliffs in 208, in which he won victory over an enemy far superior in number and firepower. The outcome of this battle played a pivotal role in the history of the Three Kingdoms. His wife Xiao Qiao was famed for her beauty. Multiple versions exist for the 7th and 8th lines of the first stanza, and the 6th and 10th lines of the second stanza, from copying errors or revisions by Dong-Po himself. The version here is from Tune Poems from Tang and Song Dynasties (An Anthology With Commentary), which makes better poetry.

p. 130: This is one of Su Dong-Po's early works, composed in 1074, when he was transferred from the position of the judge in Hangzhou to that of the governor of Mizhou. Here Chang-an refers to the Song Dynasty capitol Bianjing. The Lu Brothers refer to the poets and brothers Lu Ji and Lu Yun from the West Jin period (265-316 A.D.). They were famed for their literary talent in the West Jin capitol Luoyang when both were in their early twenties. "Ancient ideals" refer to Yao and Shun, the two legendary emperors from the early antiquity of China, who became symbols of the ideal monarch in classical Chinese culture and history.

p. 134: Su Dong-Po may have composed this tune poem in 1074. The Night of Sevens is the night when the Cowherd and the Weaving Girl (namesake of two stars separated by the Milky Way) are said to reunite each year, by crossing the bridge formed by magpies that spans the Celestial River (the Milky Way). Dong-Po adopted the title "The Night of Sevens" in keeping with the tune of this poem, but the poem may not have been composed on the Night of Sevens. Chen Ling-Ju was a friend of Dong-Po's who was demoted due to his political views. The first stanza refers to the legend of Wang Zi-Qiao (~565-549 B.C.), a prince who was said to have ascended to immortality on the Night of Sevens. The second stanza refers to the legend that the Milky Way is connected to the sea, and there are boats going back and forth between the two on schedule, accessible only to the exceptionally brave and adventurous.

p. 136: Su Dong-Po likely wrote this in 1086 or later, when he was the Master of the Imperial Academy, the prominent advisor to the emperor. East Hill refers to the abandoned military campground on a hill east of Huangzhou that Dong-Po cultivated to help support his family, also the origin of the name Dong-Po (East Hill).

p. 138: Su Dong-Po composed this poem in 1081, during his demotion in Huangzhou. Zhang Zhi-Fu was a colleague and good friend of Dong-Po's. Their poems often harmonized each other. Here Dong-Po used exactly the same rhymes as in Zhi-Fu's famous tune poem on poplar catkins. Dong-Po sent this to Zhi-Fu with a letter when Zhi-Fu traveled on official duty during the season of flying catkins. Both poems are considered masterpieces in classical Chinese poetry.

p. 142: Su Dong-Po composed this poem in late spring of 1076, during his tenure as the governor of Mizhou. He had renovated an old abandoned terrace on the northwest city wall the previous year. His brother Zi-You named it Transcendence Terrace, inspired by the ideas of Taoism's founder Lao Zi. Hearth fire was renewed each year after the Cold Food Day.

p. 144: Su Dong-Po wrote this in 1079, when he passed by Yangzhou en route to Huzhou, to where he was transferred from Xuzhou. The governor of Yangzhou held a banquet in Pingshan Hall in Dong-Po's honor, during which Dong-Po composed this poem. "The celestial old man" and "the learned governor" both refer to Dong-Po's mentor Ou-Yang Xiu, who built Pingshan Hall. Each time Dong-Po passed by Yangzhou, he went to Pingshan Hall to remember Ou-Yang Xiu. "The learned governor" and "Wispy willows in spring wind" are both taken from a tune poem by Ou-Yang Xiu.

p. 146: Qian Dai-Zhi refers to Qian Mu-Fu, a good friend of Dong-Po's. He held the position of Dai-Zhi in the imperial court, with the duty of safeguarding the national treasures.

p. 148: Su Dong-Po likely composed this tune poem three years after being demoted to Huangzhou, when the governor, Xu Jun-You, was about to be transferred from his post. They had become close friends and met up often, including on Double Ninth each year. Double Ninth was the festival on the ninth day of the ninth month in the lunar calendar, considered a very lucky day, since 九 ("nine") rhymes with久 ("a long time") in Chinese. East Xu refers to Xuzhou, where it was the custom for friends to gather at the Equestrian View Terrace on a mountain south of the city on Double Ninth. Xiang Yu annihilated the Qin Dynasty, and made Xuzhou (called Peng City at the time) his capitol in 206; he constructed the Equestrian View Terrace to watch his soldiers sport with horses that same year. South Shore (南浦) alludes to a poem by Qu Yuan, in which the god of the Yellow River parted with his beloved at South Shore. It has since come to represent the place of parting. The 7th line refers to the ancient custom for Double Ninth: breaking off a dogwood branch and wearing it in one's hair to ward off bad luck.

p. 150: "障泥" refers to the flaps draped over the horseback to guard against mud and dust. The white horse jerked Su Dong-Po because they were about to cross the stream, and the horse expected him to untie the flaps so they wouldn't get wet.

p. 152: It is unclear when So Dong-Po wrote this poem. The Taoist master Zhuang Zi likened the light of the sun to a white horse, and the human lifespan to the time it takes for the horse to cross a crack in the wall.

p. 156: In 1071, Su Dong-Po became the judge in Hang-zhou, where Chen Shu-Gu was the governor. Shu-Gu was one of Dong-Po's closest friends, with whom he often exchanged poems. During an extended trip on official business, Dong-Po missed Shu-Gu, and sent him this poem from Danyang. Lakeview Tower, Lone Mountain Temple, and Rushing Gold Gate (a water gate) were all scenic sites in Hangzhou.

p. 160: Su Dong-Po wrote this poem in 1073, while he was the judge in Hangzhou. The Seven-li Rapid was a famous part of an upper stream segment of the Qian-tang River known as the Fuchun River. One li was defined to be the length of three hundred steps in an-cient China. Yan Guang (39 B.C.-41 A.D.) was a famous hermit from the East Han period. He was a classmate of Liu Xiu, who became the emperor, and sought Yan Guang out three times, and tried in vain to engage Yan Guang in his government. The consensus was that Yan Guang refused to serve his country out of vanity.

p. 164: Su Dong-Po composed this poem in 1077, when he reunited with his brother Zi-You, and spent the Mid Autumn Festival together.

p. 166: So Dong-Po wrote this poem in 1078, when he was the governor of Xuzhou. Peng City was the ancient name for Xuzhou. Guan Pan-Pan (~785-820 A.D.) was a courtesan from the Tang Dynasty, whose lover Gener-al Zhang Shang-Shu built the Swallow Mansion for her in Xuzhou, where he was stationed. Pan-Pan was famed for her singing, dancing, and elegant charm. After

General Zhang died, Pan-Pan could not forget him, and lived alone in the Swallow Mansion. Many generations of poets were moved by her loyalty, and composed poems in her memory. Yellow Mansion was built by Dong-Po in Xuzhou, to mark the successful battle against the flooding of the Yellow River that Dong-Po led in person from the front lines.

p. 170 Su Dong-Po wrote this poem in 1074, when he saw off his friend and relative Liu Zi-Yu at Gold Mountain, an island in the Yangtze River at that time. They had been traveling together for a few months. Huan Yi (?-391 A.D.) was a master musician from the East Jin period, famous for his flute playing.

p. 172: Su Dong-Po wrote this in 1082, during his demotion in Huangzhou.

p. 174: Su Dong-Po wrote this poem in 1084, when the emperor allowed him to live in Changzhou.

Chinese Names

Bai Ju-Yi 白居易 (772-846 A.D.)

Bianjing 汴京

Bian River 汴河

Binzhou 宾州

Can Liao 参寥子, Dao Qian 道潜

Cao Cao 曹操, Lord Cao 曹公 (155-220 A.D.)

Chang-an 长安

Changzhou 常州

Chen Shu-Gu 陈述古

Chu (kingdom) 楚国

Cold Food Day 寒食日

Confucius 孔子 (~551-479 B.C.)

Crow Terrace Poetry Case 乌台诗案

Cui Hao 崔颢 (~704-754 A.D.)

Danyang 丹阳

Danzhou 儋州

Dingzhou 定州

Dong-Po Ju Shi 东坡居士, Hermit of East Hill

Dou Yi 窦毅

Du Fu 杜甫 (712-770 A.D.)

Du Mu 杜牧 (803- ~852 A.D.)

E Huang 娥皇

East Jin (period) 东晋

Emperor Shun 舜 (? - ~2208 B.C.)

Emperor Yao 尧 (~2356- ~2255 B.C.)

Equestrian View Terrace 戏马台

Ezhou 鄂州

Fuchun River 富春江

Gaotang 高唐

General Zhang Shang-Shu 张尚书

Goddesses of the Xiang River 湘灵
Golden Crane Tower 黄鹤楼
Gold Mountain 金山
Guan Pan-Pan 关盼盼 (~785-820 A.D.)
Hainan Island 海南岛
Hangzhou 杭州
Han Yu 韩愈, Tui-Zhi 退之 (768-824 A.D.)
Hanhui Terrace 涵辉楼
Huan Yi 桓伊 (?–391 A.D.)
Huang Zu 黄祖
Huangzhou 黄州
Huizhou 惠州
Kunlun Mountain 昆仑山
Jade String 玉绳
Jiangxia 江夏
Jingkou 京口
Jiujiang 九江
King of Wu Yue 吴越让王 (928-971 A.D.)
Lao Zi 老子 (604-531 B.C.)
Li Bai 李白 (701-762 A.D.)
Li Gong-Ze 李公择, Li Chang 李常
Li Shang-Yin 李商隐 (813-~858 A.D.)
Li Yuan 李渊 (566-635 A.D.)
Lingao Pavilion 临皋亭
Linping 临平
Liu Biao 刘表 (142-208 A.D.)
Liu Xiu 刘秀 (5 B.C.-57 A.D.)
Liu Yong 柳永 (~987-1053 A.D.)
Liu Yu-Xi 刘禹锡, Meng-De 梦得 (772-842 A.D.)
Liu Zi-Yu 柳子玉
Liyang 澧阳
Lord Long Qiu 龙丘子, Chen Ji-Chang 陈季常

Lord Sun 孙郎, Sun Quan 孙权 (182-252 A.D.)
Lord Xie 谢公, Xie An 谢安 (320-385 A.D.)
Lu Ji 陆机 (261-303 A.D.)
Lu Mountains 庐山
Lu Yun 陆云 (262-303 A.D.)
Luoyang 洛阳
Master of the Imperial Academy 翰林学士
Master Ying 颍师
Meishan 眉山
Meizhou 眉州
Meng Zi 孟子 (372-289 B.C.)
Mi Heng 祢衡 (173-198 A.D.)
Min E 岷峨
Mizhou 密州
North Mountain 北固山
Nu Ying 女英
Parrot Isle 鹦鹉洲
Peng City 彭城, ancient name for Xuzhou 徐州
Pingshan Hall 平山堂
Qi (kingdom) 齐国
Qian Mu-Fu 钱穆父, Qian Dai-Zhi 钱待制
Ou-Yang Xiu 欧阳修
Qu Yuan 屈原, Ling Jun 灵均 (352-281 B.C.)
Rou-Nu 柔奴
Ruzhou 汝州
Sandy Lake 沙湖
Shanzhou 陕州
Shen Yue 沈约 (441-513 A.D.)
Sichuan Province 四川省
Snow Hall 雪堂
Song Yu 宋玉, Lord Lan Tai 兰台公子 (~298 - ~222 B.C.)
South Mountains 终南山

Yan Ling 严陵, Yan Guang 严光 (39 B.C. – 41 A.D.)
Yang Tan 羊昙
Yangzhou 扬州
Yellow Mansion 黄楼
Yingzhou 颍州
Yu Heng 玉衡
Zeng Cheng 曾城
Zhang Bang-Ji 张邦基
Zhang Wo-Quan 张偓佺
Zhang Xian 张先 (990-1078 A.D.)
Zhang Zhi-Fu 章质夫
Zhou Yu 周瑜, Lord Zhou 周郎 (175-210 A.D.)
Zhu Shou-Chang 朱寿昌
Zhuang Zi 庄子 (~369 - ~286 B.C.)
Zi-You 子由, Su Zhe 苏辙 (1039-1112 A.D.)

Acknowledgments

(continued from page iv.)

Connotation Press:
"The Court Fills with Fragrance: After thirty-three years," "The Court Fills with Fragrance: Fame fits in a snail's horn," "The Water Song: Roll up brocade curtains at sunset," "The Water Song: When did the bright moon come into being," "From the River City: Ten years one alive one dead we share no light"

Kenyon Review Online:
"The Joy of Returning to Court: I dreamed I was in a little boat floating on Thunder Lake," "Journey through Incense: A crystal night untouched by dust"

Kyoto Journal:
"From the River City: I saw it all and woke from the drunken dream," "Trimmed Magnolia: A pair of dragons rise face to face," "The Fisherman"

Salamander Magazine:
"Sand of the Washing Stream: Soft grass and flat sedge freshen after rain," "Sand of the Washing Stream: The wind flies fast clouds low over the water"

Willow Springs:
"Calming the Wind and Waves: Ignore the sounds piercing trees and beating leaves," "From the River City: An old man lets loose some youthful wildness," "To the Bridegroom: A fledging swallow flies into the

mansion"

I am indebted to Bill Porter/Red Pine for invaluable discussions on the alternative translations of the original Chinese poems over the period of October 2015 to January 2018, and for holding my English translations to high standards in fidelity and poetry. I am grateful to Richard Jarrette for helpful comments and suggestions on an earlier draft of the book manuscript in May 2015.

About the Translator

Yun Wang is the author of two poetry books (*The Book of Totality*, Salmon Poetry Press, 2015; and *The Book of Jade*, Winner of the 15th Nicholas Roerich Poetry Prize, Story Line Press, 2002), two poetry chapbooks (*Horse by the Mountain Stream*, Word Palace Press, 2016; *The Carp*, Bull Thistle Press, 1994). Wang's poems have been published in numerous literary journals, including *The Kenyon Review, Prairie Schooner, Cimarron Review, Salamander Magazine, Green Mountains Review,* and *International Quarterly*. Her translations of classical Chinese poetry have been published in *The Kenyon Review Online, Salamander Magazine, Poetry Canada Review, Willow Springs, Kyoto Journal, Connotation Press,* and elsewhere. Wang is a cosmologist at California Institute of Technology.

Companions for the Journey Series

༄

Inspirational work by well-known writers in a small-
book format designed to be carried along on your
journey through life.

Volume 26
Precious Mirror
Kobun Otogawa
Translated by Gary Young
978-1-945680-21-1   100 pages

Volume 25
Unexpected Development
Klaus Merz
Translated by Marc Vincenz
978-1-945680-14-4   142 pages

Volume 24
Poetics of Wonder: Passage to Mogdor
Alberto Ruy-Sánchez
Translated by Rhonda Dahl Buchanan
978-1-935210-55-9   156 pages

Volume 23
Searching for Guan Yin
Sarah E. Truman
978-1-935210-28-3   288 pages

Volume 22

Illustrations by Michael Hofmann
1-893996-49-2   70 pages

Volume 10
Because of the Rain: Korean Zen Poems
Translated by Won-Chung Kim and Christopher Merrill
1-893996-44-1   96 pages

Volume 9
Pilgrim of the Clouds
Poems and Essays from Ming Dynasty China
Translated by Jonathan Chaves
1-893996-39-5   192 pages

Volume 8
The Unswept Path: Contemporary American Haiku
Edited by John Brandi and Dennis Maloney
1-893996-38-7   220 pages

Volume 7
Lotus Moon: The Poetry of Rengetsu
Translated by John Stevens
Afterword by Bonnie Myotai Treace
1-893996-36-0   132 pages

Volume 6
A Zen Forest: Zen Sayings
Translated by Soioku Shigematsu
Preface by Gary Snyder
1-893996-30-1   120 pages

Volume 5